Philosophy and Medical Welfare

ROYAL INSTITUTE OF PHILOSOPHY LECTURE SERIES: 23
SUPPLEMENT TO *PHILOSOPHY* 1988

EDITED BY

J. M. Bell and Susan Mendus

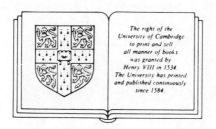

The right of the
University of Cambridge
to print and sell
all manner of books
was granted by
Henry VIII in 1534.
The University has printed
and published continuously
since 1584.

CAMBRIDGE UNIVERSITY PRESS

CAMBRIDGE   NEW YORK
NEW ROCHELLE   MELBOURNE   SYDNEY

Published by the Press Syndicate of the University of Cambridge
The Pitt Building, Trumpington Street, Cambridge, CB2 1RP
32 East 57th Street, New York, NY 10022, USA.
10 Stamford Street, Oakleigh, Melbourne 3166, Australia

Library of Congress catalogue card number: 88-17059

British Library Cataloguing in Publication Data

Philosophy and medical welfare: supplement
   to philosophy 1988
   1. Public health services. Ethical aspects.
   I. Bell, J. M.   II. Mendus, Susan
   III. Philosophy
   174'.2

   ISBN 0-521-36856-1

Library of Congress Cataloguing in Publication Data

Philosophy and medical welfare/edited by J. M. Bell and Susan Mendus.
   p. cm.—(Royal Institute of Philosophy lecture series; 23)
   Papers originally presented at a conference at the University of York in
Sept. 1987.
   "Supplement to Philosophy 1988."
   ISBN 0-521-36856-1
   1. Social Medicine—Congresses. 2. Philosophy—Congresses.
I. Bell, J. M. (John Martin), 1944–   . II. Mendus, Susan.
III. Philosophy. 1988 (Supplement)   IV. Series: Royal Institute of Philoso-
phy lectures; v. 23.
RA418.P48   1988
362.1—dc19   88-17059
                                                                          CIP

ISBN 0 521 36856-1 (pbk.)

Printed and bound by
Adlard & Son Limited
Leatherhead, Surrey, and Letchworth, Hertfordshire

Contents

Preface

The papers contained in this volume originated in contributions to the Royal Institute of Philosophy Conference on 'Philosophy and Medical Welfare' held at the University of York in September 1987.

Participants at the Conference included doctors, nurses, administrators, scientists and others working in the field of health care, as well as academics from the disciplines of economics, politics and philosophy.

Our thanks to the Royal Institute of Philosophy for financial support both for the Conference and with the making of this volume; and to Mrs Janet Yates who prepared the typsecript for publication.

Martin Bell
Susan Mendus

Department of Philosophy
University of York

Preface

List of Contributors

Professor Martin Hollis, School of Economics and Social Studies, University of East Anglia.

Dr Robert Goodin, Department of Government, University of Essex.

Dr Michael Lockwood, Department of External Studies, University of Oxford.

Professor John Broome, Department of Economics, University of Bristol.

Dr John Harris, Centre for Social Ethics and Policy, University of Manchester.

Professor Albert Weale, School of Economics and Social Studies, University of East Anglia.

Professor Alan Williams, Department of Economics and Related Studies, University of York.

A Death of One's Own

MARTIN HOLLIS

The wish to have a death of one's own is growing ever rarer. Only a while yet and it will be just as rare to have a death of one's own as it is already to have a life of one's own.

Rainer Maria Rilke

Rilke's remark conjures up an officious array of well-meaning persons bent on completing our orderly passage from cradle to grave. They tidy our files cosily about us, inject us with extreme unction and slide us into the warm embrace of the undertaker. At the forefront of the array stands the doctor, part mechanic and part priest. His main task is to repair the living with resources whose effective and impartial allocation is a chief topic of medical ethics. But his role is not that of an impartial allocator: his patients want his partisan support. This builds a moral tension into a role played out where system meets patient, and one made instructively plain in the care of the dying. The system no doubt prefers death to be cheap and orderly but this thought may not move someone like Rilke wanting a death of his own. The doctor is then caught between his general duty to patients at large and his particular duty to the patient in front of him, a tension tautened for a Hippocratic promoter of health and life by a patient in search of an exit.

To put flesh on the theme, let us start with an awkward case for the doctor. George is an old man, a widower, in hospital after a stroke. Although fairly well recovered, he is still fragile and has poor balance. But he is clear-headed, especially about his wish to go home. He says firmly that he could manage on his own; and so he probably could, if he had enough support. Otherwise there is a real danger of his falling, fracturing a leg and being unable to summon help. There is a risk of hypothermia. He may easily become dirty, unkempt, emaciated and dehydrated, since it is not plain that he can dress, toilet and feed himself for long. He may not manage to comply with his medication. He might perhaps even become a risk to others by leaving his fire unattended or causing a gas explosion. None of this would be worrying, if there was a supporting cast. But his house is not suited to his condition. His only relative is his daughter, living elsewhere, with her own job and family and not willing to take George on. His neighbours are unfriendly. Social Services can offer something—perhaps a home help, meals on wheels, a laundry service, day care, an alarm service. But this does not truly cover nights and weekends and, anyway, George is liable not to eat the meals and not to accept the day care. Meanwhile the advice from social services is that he should stay in hospital. It is good advice for the further reason that there will be no second chance. Often one can allow a patient a try at looking after himself, knowing that he can be scooped up and returned to hospital, if necessary. But George is too fragile and too alone for this to be a promising option. Yet he is in no doubt that he wants to go home and denies that he needs any of the missing support.

This situation was described to me by an experienced GP as one commonly encountered and ethically difficult.[1] He added two questions. How much self-determination should George be allowed, given that his insight is poor? How much responsibility does the doctor shoulder, if he colludes with George's wishes? Both questions sound easy, if one begins by disputing their assumption that they can be posed primarily from the doctor's point of view. Or so I supposed, until I tried the familiar philosophical tactic of challenging the assumptions and found that the still waters run awkwardly deep. In what follows, I shall open with George's point of view and try to extract a line which gives the doctor clear guidance. Having duly failed, I shall then address the tension between system and patient as claimants on the doctor's integrity, before finally reverting to George's own wishes for his life or death.

The first question was how much self-determination George should be allowed, given that his insight is poor. As a preliminary, the story, as told, does not guarantee that George's insight is poor at all. It could be that he has a pretty shrewd idea that he will not last long on his own but simply wants to go home to die. Being also shrewd enough to know that he cannot expect the doctor's co-operation on those terms, he takes on the conventional patient's role in a well-tried dramatic dialogue between confident patient and concerned doctor. It is both polite and politic to offer the doctor clean hands by persuading him that the patient has the determination to cope. It is both polite and politic for the doctor to collude in what is, after all, not exactly the doctor's business, once he has been offered enough to satisfy any later enquiry into negligence. Under the surface of the conventional dialogue another has been conducted. George's questions about his true condition, asked and unasked, have been answered and advice given. George has rejected the advice, absolving the doctor of private and public responsibility. Honour has been satisfied on both sides.

I raise this possibility as a way of ushering one what one might call a decent liberalism. Traditionally the doctor's role is attended with more

[1] I would like to thank Dr Brian Cole warmly both for this starting point and for help in seeing what might be done with it philosophically. I am also grateful to Albert Weale for comments on an earlier draft.

paternalism than a liberal doctor may relish. The liberal reminds us that today's doctor is no longer God and should not play God. He is the patient's servant, not his master. If George really did want to live out a full, self-sufficient life and was suffering from illusions, brought on perhaps by resentment at the humiliations of hospital routine, then the doctor might have a duty to be obstructive. But a good servant accepts his master's wishes and, in so far as George is weary of the world, the doctor is not his judge. Doubts about George'a autonomy, a liberal would say, should be resolved in George's favour and a discreet way found of avoiding scandal. George's insight is not *outrageously* poor and there is a chance that it is not poor at all.

The crux for this liberal line does not depend on whether the doctor has a formal power to keep George in hospital or is merely giving authoritative advice which he can make prevail. Whichever kind of authority it is, he should use it to uphold George's genuine wishes. This directive applies broadly even where George is under some illusion about his likely power to cope but is not exactly brimming with the will to live. The doctor's moral responsibility is to be supportive when he can, and *in loco parentis* only when he must.

We can distinguish two routes to this result. One starts by thinking of patients as bodies and of doctors as mechanics. George has, so to speak, brought his rickety old Ford to the garage with a big end gone and been told, that, although pretty clapped out, it would do a few thousand more miles, if left in for further repairs. Some garages are gleaming hi-tech affairs, which strip the car down in a flash and will not give it back until the bemused owner has signed an open cheque for whatever the garage sees fit to do. The medical equivalent of these motoring pits are hospital wards ruled by lordly consultants with acolytes, who strip away the patient's identity and turn him into an object before pretending to consult him on the technology of his health. But there are liberal garages too. There the owner is given an assessment before the dismantling starts and, even if nudged with a spot of advice, is left to make the decision. What makes this traditionally liberal is less its general view that, as J. S. Mill put it, there is a circle round each individual human being, which it is not the job of government or anyone else to invade, and more its particular presumption (also to be found in Mill) that a person is a mind, who owns a physical machine whose disposal is up to the owner.

The liberal line becomes trickier, if, as has become fashionable of late, one reverts to the ancient view that patients are not bodies but *persons,* and adds that a person is not a mind lodged in a body like a pilot in a vessel or motorist in a car. This subverts the idea that the doctor is just a mechanic and hence subverts one neat way of denying that the doctor is God. The other liberal route to granting the patient's autonomy thus starts from an idea of respect for *persons*. For all its greater current plausibility, it is stonier, however, and I am not sure that it gets there. Here are some of the complications.

George's chances of coping on his own seemed at first to depend merely on the support available for his rickety physical machine. But, if George is thought of as a *person,* we shall have to notice that psychological and social factors matter too. To discuss the social factors would take me too far afield. So let me just say that George's chances of recovering manageably from a stroke may vary with his class, gender, income and previous occupation, and that strokes may belong in a mysterious category, along with, for example, cot deaths and schizophrenia, where it looks as if social factors may even be causal. Meanwhile there is the obvious social point that he would get on better if he had friendly neighbours. In brief, the likely health of *persons* cannot be assessed in social isolation.

More directly relevant are the psychological factors. George's chances depend on his state of mind—his desires, beliefs and strength of will—which the doctor who treats George as a person must take into account. An instant complication is that the doctor's diagnosis or prognosis can affect George's chances. For an extreme case reflect on the common tale that in cultures which believe in witchcraft the knowledge that he has been cursed is enough to make a man curl up and die. In George's case there is an obvious risk that, in establishing his chances of survival, the doctor will upset his precarious balance and thus improve his insight at the expense of his health. In general the liberal view is that knowledge is always a Good Thing and, in general, I shall not doubt it. But even a liberal admits some exceptions, where true beliefs are a handicap. For instance the skater may be better off unaware that the ice is thin, the tightrope walker unaware that he is crossing a snake pit, the soldier unaware that the ground is mined. George may need his self-confidence and a doctor, who believes in improving people's insight, may be something of a health risk.

The point becomes less quirky in relation to desires, as opposed to beliefs. Having it borne in on him just how lonely, friendless and helpless he is can seriously damage George's will to live. The doctor cannot assess the situation by, so to speak, hidden camera and one-way mirror alone. He must interact with George, must probe his determination or apathy and, in short, must prod the roots of the plant to see how well they withstand prodding. This is also a comment on the earlier thought that George may be wholly clear about consequences but too diplomatic to say so: the doctor cannot act on the mere possibility that it is so. If George started with an unresolved mixture of hope for an independent life and weariness of a lonely one, he may well finish with a newly defined wish to go home to die. To put it too starkly, no doubt, respect for persons threatens sometimes to mean killing them off.

It is rapidly becoming unclear whether we are concerned with George's wants or George's interests. Which of the two is indicated by the maxim that patients should be treated as persons? The easier answer is the economist's: let there be consumer sovereignty for George's *wants*. If he still wants to go home after becoming clear about the risks, then the doctor has no business to obstruct him further. A merit of the answer is that it avoids having to tangle with the awkward concept of interests. Who can say that it is in George's interest to drift on into an institutionalized decline rather than to shorten his loneliness by returning home? The doctor is to probe the difference between considered and unconsidered wants. Having established what George truly wants, he need not worry about whether the preferred outcome is in George's interests. Autonomy, in other words, goes with considered wants, not real interests. This is the liberal attitude which I had in mind for the initial question of how much self-determination George should be allowed. The doctor is not to set up as an authority on the riddle of existence: on that each patient is his own sovereign consumer.

The suggestion, generalized, is that the doctor's role should be patient-centred, with patients sovereign and doctors their servants. A death of one's own is the ultimate in consumer choice. When generalized thus, however, this version of liberalism runs into difficulty. I shall try to show first that patient-centredness is not a clear guide to action and then that, even when it is, it may not be a good guide.

A Scottish doctor recently landed himself in trouble by adopting a novel approach to the problem of when to stop treating senile patients who catch something lethal like pneumonia. He began taking instructions from his patients at an earlier age, when they were old and thinking about getting older. He asked them what they would wish done, if they became senile and the problem arose. Many replied firmly that they would wish to be allowed to die in those circumstances, and wrote it down as a, so to speak, penultimate will and testament. The doctor reasoned that, since one cannot consult patients with senile dementia, the next best thing is to consult their former selves. The British Medical Association, however, would have none of this. The responsibility for a senile patient, it said, is and must remain the doctor's. He should consult relatives but the presumption must remain that patients wish to live and that doctors are there for the purpose. The patient's younger self cannot be an authoritative voice.

The BMA was, I think, rather careful not to say too much. There are some discreet conventions about the withholding of treatment for patients where prospect of a fair quality of life is gone beyond recall, and the BMA said nothing on this score. Its objection was to involving the patient's former self. It has to be an objection on behalf not of the patient's wants but of his interests. It is no good arguing that the senile patient would *want* to live on, if able to consider the matter rationally, since the problem arises only when the patient cannot consider the matter rationally. The objection has to be that the patient's earlier utterance mis-states the patient's later *interests*. The Scottish doctor might seem to have the stronger ground, if one believes that a patient-centred approach is to be one governed by the patient's *wants,* since he at least has an earlier statement of a *want* to go by. But one suspects that even he is not acting on the mere fact of a want expressed but on his own belief that death has become in the patient's interests.

Thus prompted, we should notice that the classic liberal spokesman on the sovereignty of the individual words the case in terms of interests. The argument of Mill's *On Liberty* is that it is in our *interests* to be left to pursue our own good in our own way (so long as we do not interfere with the liberty of others). In *The Principles of Political Economy* he maintains that individuals are the best judges of their own *interests.* This at once raises a question about whether individuals' *wants* are sovereign, when they conflict with their interests. Mill gives a clear answer—No. In *On Liberty* he insists that the only liberty worth the name is that of pursuing our own good in our own way and argues that neither legal nor physical force may be used to compel or obstruct this pursuit. But he has no scruples about applying social pressure to ensure that we use the liberty to achieve the individuality and autonomy, which he holds to be in our interests, whatever our foolish wishes to the contrary. In the *Principles* (Book V, Chapter 11) he considers seven exceptions to the general maxim that individuals are the best judges of their own interests and bids government take action in each of them to make sure that what is done is truly in individual's interests. Among them are cases where the individuals concerned are not mature and sane adults in full possession of their faculties, and where an individual attempts 'to decide irrevocably now what will be in his interest at some future time'. The Scottish doctor can still invoke Mill against the BMA but only by arguing that the senile patient's younger self remains a reliable guide to the *interests* of someone who has ceased to be a sane adult in possession of his faculties and whose 'own good' is to die.

Death is, in general, an awkward case for a liberal debate about what is in someone's interests. If death is the end of a person, then it closes his profit and loss account, making it hard to maintain that he will be better off, if he no longer exists. Even the thought that his life would be in the red, were he around to live it, becomes awkward with senile dementia. On the other hand, if death is not the end, then who knows how to adjust the profit and loss account for another world? Yet a fully patient-centred approach would need a view on these enigmas. Perhaps that is why the Exit Society, which advocates euthanasia and helps people in search of a death of their own, cannot persuade the medical profession that doctors should be as obliging about death as about life. It is worth noting, however, that societies vary. In Holland, for instance, exits seem to be very much easier to come by—a fact worth noting not only because more old people are living on to a stage where life is a burden but also because AIDS will soon be reaping the young in numbers too large to be furtive about.

At any rate, my point is that a patient-centred approach cannot avoid tangling with questions of *interests* as soon as patients start wanting what is bad for their health. This is not to say that good health is always an overriding interest—doctors are sometimes asked to support people doing dangerous or exhausting tasks which shorten their lives. But no doctor is required to help masochists suffer more pain in the name of consumer sovereignty. The most libertarian version of a liberal-inspired patient-centredness on offer is one which gives the patient the benefit of the doubt when it is not clear that his wants are in his interests.

Patient-centredness is thus not the enemy of paternalism that one might suppose. It invites us to decide in the patient's interests but leaves the doctor often the better judge of them. All the same, I imagine that sympathies still lie with George, old, lonely, uncared for and wanting release. The first question was how much self-determination he should be allowed, given that his insight is poor. Treating George as a person will, I imagine, be held to imply only that the doctor should make sure that his insight is not so poor as to frustrate his clear interests. So far, presumably, George goes home.

But I have almost commanded this answer by asking about a single patient and exploiting the obvious attractions of patient-centredness as a guide to medicine. The other question was how much responsibility the doctor shoulders, if he colludes with George's wishes. A natural thought is that, if the answer to the first question is to give George the decision, then the doctor must be morally in the clear for the purposes of the second. But, on reflection, it is not so simple. Even a patient-centred approach saddles the doctor with moral responsibilities which are not exhausted by serving George's interests. I open my case by asking which patient is to be at the centre of a patient-centred approach.

It is time that the doctor had a name too. Resisting a revealing temptation to call him Dr Smith, I shall christen him Henry. (In what follows Henry is a hospital doctor overseeing George's treatment and discharge. But, since the moral relationship which I want to discuss is a professional yet personal one better typified by a GP, he can be thought of as George's GP also. This elasticity, I trust, will not spoil the argument.) It is a trick of the example to suggest that Henry is involved only as George's medical adviser and that only Henry is involved in the decision. Henry has other patients beside George and belongs to a medical profession most of whose patients are not Henry's. Equally I blanked out other people concerned with George, notably the social services department, but they are still in the wings and they too have other clients and commitments. None of this matters to George, seeking the patient-centred solution which fits in with his wishes, but it is bound to weigh with Henry. Morally speaking, collusion will not be an isolated act.

George is occupying a hospital bed. There are other people waiting for beds and George does not really need one. At first sight this is not Henry's problem, partly because it is not his fault that there is a lack of outside support to keep George going and more generally because ordinary hospital doctors and GPs are not responsible for the overall allocation of resources. But this is too formal a way of looking at a doctor's responsibilities. If Henry is an experienced and respected GP, he has a *de facto* power to call up social service support or to secure hospital beds, while his credit remains good. His credit is staked on every case and depends on his not staking it too casually. He can mortgage it for any one patient but, if his fellow professionals do not agree that the case merited the resources by comparison with other cases, it will be that much harder for Henry to secure help for his next patient. Hence Henry's considered pronouncement on George may have costs and benefits to Henry's other patients. To serve *all* his patients he needs a good reputation among those who allocate resources which cannot meet all claims by all doctors. George, let us assume, simply wants the best result for himself. Henry aims more widely at the best for all his patients. These aims can conflict.

Moreover Henry is not solely the champion of his own patients. He has a doctor's concern for all the sick, shared with fellow doctors and with others in the work of promoting health. That opens up an interesting ambiguity in the notion of patient-centred care. Should each doctor care for his own patients (and, more broadly, each professional for his own parish)? Or should each behave as a member of a group whose aim is the good of all patients? These alternatives do not yield the same result. Just as Henry's 100 per cent effort on George's behalf may do what is best for George at the expense of Henry's other patients, so Henry's 100 per cent commitment to his own patients may be at the expense of other patients. Similarly, a powerful consultant, administrator or health team can get more than proportional resources for their own parish if their own parish is what counts. Patient-centredness is ambiguous on the point. Offhand one is inclined to say that the care a patient receives should depend not on who he is, where he lives or who his doctor is, but on what he needs. That suggests a sort of Kantian universality, bidding us look on all cases evenly from some central vantage point. On the other hand, the obvious universal Kantian imperative to each doctor or carer is 'Do your best for your patients' and this comes with the tempting utilitarian thought that since each doctor has a personal bond with his own patients and each professional with his own patch, the total amount of good care resulting will be greater.

If Henry is an experienced, effective doctor who knows how to work the system better than most, then equality of patients' need seems to mean that he should *not* do his best for his patients. To block this odd conclusion, we might try envisaging the care network as a system of checks and balances. Henry is to do his best for his own patients but other professionals, with their rather different concerns, do their best to stop him getting away with unfair allocations. That offers a promising rationale for the division of caring labour, given an ideal allocation of resources (including professional skills). If the doctor can count on social work support but only when his request for it is reasonable in relation to other requests, then we perhaps have something like a game where each player can go flat out in the knowledge that enforced rules of fair play will stop him and others gaining unjust advantages. The best efforts of each in his own parish can then sum to the best which the system can deliver as a whole.

But this is to take a very idealized view of the social world about us. In George's case, it supposes that the social service department has proper resources, so that it can support George at no cost to its other more desperate clients, if the request for support is reasonable. In practice social service departments are sure to be stretched thinner than this. Being under-resourced and, most unfairly, the target of political suspicion or hostility, they can do a job which will withstand public scrutiny in case of disaster and official enquiry only if they take on less cases than ideally would be for the best. As I presented George's story, social services were offering some support but probably not enough to keep him going in earnest. Although this may have reflected their view that, given the lack of family and friends, he should stay in hospital, it may also have been because they could not spare the resources for major support, given the other claims on them. At any rate let us suppose it so and ask how that affects Henry's ethical responsibilities.

The general puzzle is one of professional duty in a world of imperfect compliance. It is not one of legal obligation, since Henry can see to it that his back is covered whatever he does. He can steer George either back home or back into his hospital bed and cover himself by the wording of his professional judgment. Ethically, however, we still want to know how much responsibility is his if he steers George home, knowing that the social work support really available is not really enough. It is not his responsibility to provide enough support to free George's hospital bed with a clear conscience. But he has a moral decision to make and he is answerable for it in a way which George is not and which is not trumped by George's wish to go home. He might consider, for instance, encouraging George to go home partly because this is one way of putting pressure on those who allocate the budget to social services. This would be for the future benefit of others in need but hardly for the present benefit of George. This sort of consideration is endemic in the ethics of professional roles when played out among roles which mesh imperfectly, and it is one on which patient-centredness gives no guidance.

A final ambiguity about 'patient-centred' is found by asking whether it means 'answerable to the patient'. The initial reaction is probably that it does. The doctor–patient relationship is usually deemed one-to-one, in that it is a confidential relation of trust between a doctor and a patient with a right to his undivided commitment. But a couple of examples will show that there is more to it. In the days before syphilis was curable and Wassermann tests required before marriage, a New York doctor diagnosed syphilis in a patient and advised telling his fiancée. The patient refused. Recently (although it may be just a new urban legend) a London doctor diagnosed AIDS in a patient, who demanded utter confidentiality, and was presented a few months later with the man's unsuspecting wife, radiantly pregnant. Both women happened also to be patients of the respective doctors but this point only focuses the ambiguity about which patient to centre upon. The broader question is whether even a patient-centred practice is not answerable to a wider tribunal. The doctor is not like a priest upholding the secrecy of the confessional in the face of enquiries by the temporal authorities. He is an agent licensed by that state, akin less to a priest than to a social worker who is explicitly the state's appointee, wielding its authority even in seemingly personal relations with clients. The doctor is answerable to the community at large and, although it is relevant whether or not syphilis and AIDS are legally notifiable diseases, his professional conscience is not fully absolved by this test. How much responsibility does Henry shoulder if he colludes with George's wishes? The question is incomplete: how much responsibility *to whom*?

It has emerged by now, I hope, that if we try for something patient-centred, to the effect that the doctor's duty is to his patient, the idea is thoroughly ambiguous. Even concentrating on the particular patient of the immediate case we find that the duty is to serve the patient's interests as a person rather than his declared wants for his physical machine. Liberal notions of autonomy leave the patient's wishes the benefit of the doubt as a guide to his interests but override them when his insight is clearly lacking. Meanwhile patient-centredness cannot be construed thus one-to-one. Henry is answerable for more people than George and to more people than George. He is responsible at least for his other patients; perhaps, as a member of the caring professions for the overall welfare of those in need of care. Equally he is responsible not only to George and other patients but also to fellow professionals and ultimately the community at large. As soon as resources are short or roles mesh imperfectly, Henry's best efforts for George have a price paid elsewhere. 'Patient-centred' starts with George but cannot mean simply 'George-centred' and gives no guidance on where to stop. George is still inescapably Henry's patient. So far I have turned a simple plea by an old and lonely widower for a death of his own into an intricate set of questions about Henry's duties. That is rough on George but, all the same, I propose to say a bit more about professional integrity as a factor in medical ethics before returning to death as a proper exercise of consumer sovereignty.

This difficult notion comes with some philosophical baggage which needs to be unloaded. Integrity, as a general moral concept, is commonly invoked as an objection to consequentialist ethics: even if it would save the Health Service a pile of money to let George die off quietly, Henry should refuse to be party to such base calculation. This admonition may be made from either of two points of view. One belongs to the kind of deontological or duty-based ethics which opposes principle to consequence and bids us do right and damn the consequences. From this point of view the Hippocratic oath is a sort of categorical medical imperative which forbids doctors all compromise with lack of resources or any other obstacle to the patient's good health. Integrity demands acting on pure principle with the moral consistency of a rhinoceros. My short comment is that principle and consequence cannot be so starkly opposed. On the one hand utilitarians are applying a principle when they adopt whatever solution makes for the greater welfare of the greater number. On the other there are always questions or whether a principle is appropriate to a situation and of how it is to be applied—questions which demand care for results. Hence integrity does not provide independent leverage on what is right or best to do. It demands only that, having identified the right or best thing to do, the agent goes ahead and does it.

The other common use of integrity is to appeal against all systematic ethics, whether of principle or of consequence. The *locus classicus* is the existentialist idea of authenticity which forbids the agent to accept *any* general guidance in advance of a situation, on pain of 'bad faith'. Sartre's *Existentialism and Humanism* insists that an authentic moral agent recognizes that he chooses even his feelings or conscience; and a scarcely less radical rejection of all guides to moral choice can be found in Peter Winch's essay on 'Moral Integrity'. My equally short comment

11

is that we can agree in refusing to let the doctor hide behind an unexamined conscience but cannot possibly construe professional integrity as *carte blanche* for a professional to do whatever he finds most 'authentic' at the moment of choice.

That leaves two unmistakable tensions involved in the notion of professional integrity, both concerned with the relation of self to role. One has to do with conflicts between a doctor's personal beliefs and the demands of his office. The other has to do with the degree for which he is personally responsible, when the duties of his role are overriden by other pressures.

Cases where personal belief can conflict with official duty are easy to find. The Catholic doctor's patients may include a woman in search of an abortion. If he personally regards abortion as murder and the abetting of abortion as the abetting of murder, how helpful does his role order him to be and how helpful should he therefore be? There are terminal patients in great pain who want only to die. Is a doctor who, personally, believes in euthanasia professionally bound to resist their death? There are ways of muting such conflicts. If he will not deal in abortions, no doubt he can refer the patient to a doctor who will. With a terminal patient he need not strive officiously to keep alive. But, even when muted, conflicts remain. In some authorities most doctors are anti-abortion. Does that imply a duty on each of them to pocket their consciences? Letting patients die is not always distinct from killing them. If one supposes that justice calls for similar treatment in any part of the country and from any doctor, can we countenance any luck of the draw in death?

The dilemmas of professional integrity are distinct both from personal dilemmas (shall I betray my country or my friend?) and from professional dilemmas (shall Henry improve George's insight at the expense of his health?) They cross the line between personal and professional. Presumably no one thinks that the doctor should hang up his conscience along with his hat and obey all possible orders by the authority which hands out his stethoscope. In that case he might as well take the job of medical assistant to a team of torturers. But integrity can seem so much a personal notion that the opposite view is tempting. Should he ever compromise his private conscience and, if so, when and why?

The easy part of the answer is that private conscience is not infallible and where it is just another term for personal convictions, not safe from bigotry. A doctor may not eject patients from his surgery as he might visitors from his living room. He cannot refuse them on grounds of their race, sex, religion or politics. But, on the other hand, total moral neutrality is not what we ask of doctors. We expect them to uphold a professional code, whose rationale is their special situation in relation to a broader ethic of concern for others. The broader ethic cannot be wholly bland and its special application to medicine is bound to conflict from time to time with what a doctor personally thinks right. Mismatch can occur in both directions. For example official guidance for doctors on abortion, on severely handicapped infants, on patients long comatose and on the incurably senile can strike some as too strict and others as too lax. Then there will be tension because we need the doctor's personal moral commitment but not too much of it.

The same goes for the other kind of tension, when scarcity of resources interferes with the doctor's duty. The National Health Service had hoped originally to avoid this difficulty by giving doctors a free hand in prescribing what they thought best. But it is clear by now that the medical task is expanding, not shrinking, and cannot possibly be fully resourced. Two typical ways of applying the cork are to limit the doctors' efforts (for instance by restricting the list of prescribable drugs or by letting queues form) and to put decisions about allocation in non-medical hands (as with the rationing of kidney machines by committees of citizens). However it is done, doctors are then asked to acquiesce in what they may think a betrayal of their calling. They may wonder whether they are absolved from guilt, when their patients die of treatable renal failure, by the undoubted fact that they did not decide the allocation between health and roadbuilding.

What makes such tensions morally distinctive, in my view, is that the ethics of role are a *tertium quid* in the dispute between agent-neutral ethics and agent-relative ethics. An agent-neutral ethics is one of the golden rule, Kantian or even utilitarian kind, which holds that an action is right for me if and only if it would be right for *anyone* so placed. An agent-relative ethics maintains that each of us is morally peculiar, for instance because we are each morally constituted by some personal project which informs our lives, and hence that different people should behave differently in the same situation. It is not an easy dispute to umpire because both sides nuance their positions. Just as the golden rule on car parking need not be 'No parking' but 'No parking on yellow lines' or 'on Saturdays' or 'by lorries', so there can presumably be imperatives addressed to doctors. Conversely agent-relative theories tend to be surprisingly systematic about the claims of those near and dear to us, like family, friends, neighbours and compatriots. That makes it correspondingly unclear that the dilemmas of self and role are truly a *tertium quid*. All the same a doctor's dilemma seems to me resistant to both pulls. In the universalizing direction, there is no problem where doctors merely have a special *duty* to do what people at large are *permitted* to do. But what if they sometimes have a duty to kill patients when the universal rule is 'thou shalt not kill'? In the particularizing direction, there would be no problem if doctors could express themselves in their practice in whatever way suited their own project in life. But this is absolutely not what we intend by a licence to practise medicine. To become a doctor is to accept a code which may be doctor-relative but is certainly not relative to the individual doctor. There is a *tertium quid* as soon as we think of role in general terms and self in particular terms, thus creating a threat of incommensurability.

The shoe pinches harder for some professions than others. For example, social workers are professionally expected to make personal friends with their clients so as to wield their statutory authority in a fully informed way. This injects an ambiguity, bordering on a duplicity, into a role which would not work as well without it. In their assessment of whether a child is at risk of abuse and needs removing to a place of safety, they have to mortgage their personal judgment, in the knowledge that it is not possible to remove in total all the children for whom there is a genuine risk. Yet the system would not work, and more children would be abused and killed, if social workers refused to live with this constant threat to their integrity. Doctors are less exposed, because they are protected by the white coat of clinical judgment. But it is not a coat of infallibility and what it covers is often not solely a scientific assessment. Here too the role involves special duties and hence moral decisions in a professional capacity, whose ethical basis is obscure.

But if I shuffle the paper much longer George will simply die of old age. So let us draw the threads together, answer the question about Henry's responsibility, if he colludes with George, and lets the poor fellow go home at last. I have been offering an oblique comment on a natural approach to medical ethics, which goes, so to speak, top down. One starts with a broad aim for the system, like maximizing welfare subject to constraints of justice, and tries to translate it into policies for allocating resources and applying them to individual patients. I do not think this is a false approach and I have not tried to belittle the problems it identifies, which are typically to do with scarcity of resources and the need to weigh the claims of medicine against other priorities. My comment is that, however well one works things out top down, there is an ineliminable moral friction where top down meets bottom up. Where policy meets patient, the doctor has moral choices to make which no code of medical ethics can reduce to routine. Since a system of care is to be judged finally at its point of delivery, it is crucial to think about it from bottom up as well as from top down.

Considerations of justice and welfare are, in the main, impersonal, impartial and universal. Patients, in the main, expect their doctors to take a particular, personal and partial interest in them. Caught with Kant and Bentham on his bookshelf, Hippocrates in his waiting room and the ombudsman on the telephone, the doctor finds his role under-scripted, his ethics ambiguous and his integrity prone to disintegrate. The doctor–patient relationship is more than a *bricolage* of morally untidy choices but less than a systematic application of moral philosophy. It can be guided by an ethics of resource allocation but there is an endemic friction where system meets patient. Medicine has more to it than applying decision theory to diseases.

How much responsibility does the doctor shoulder if he colludes with George's wishes? What he should do no doubt varies with George's insight but the doctor's responsibility is constant. To collude with *very* poor insight is to act on the proposition that George is better off dead. To collude with *very* good insight is to endorse George's choice to die. To collude with hazy insight is to stand aside by letting doubt demand the benefit of doubt. Whichever it is, Henry has made a choice and staked his integrity on it. I imagine that most doctors will think it best to let George go and will find this responsibility easiest to shoulder. Indeed, I think that they must, as more people live longer into a fragile and confused old age. But responsibility is not here lessened on the ground that letting die is not killing. Having learnt to postpone death, we have set ourselves problems of when to cut short the losses of an extended life. We have a collective responsibility for what Henry decides but Henry is responsible for his decision. Although he can cover his back by recording a clinical judgment that George's insight and prospects were adequate, he knows that there is more to the moral question than clinical judgment.

At any rate, George goes home. He remains on his doctor's conscience as he is carried out a month later to a forgotten grave. But so he would have done also, languishing on in a hospital bed. Without hoping to make it easier to see in the twilight, let me end with a patient-centred prayer, also from Rilke:

> O Herr, gib jedem seinen eignen Tod,
> Das Sterben, das aus jedem Leben geht,
> Darin er Liebe hatte, Sinn und Not.

Even when a death of one's own is a poor consumer choice, it is a proper exercise of human dignity.

Heroic Measures and False Hopes

ROBERT E. GOODIN

The precise application of the term 'heroic measures' in the discourse of medicine and medical ethics is somewhat uncertain. What counts and what does not is, at the margins, a perpetually contentious issue. Basically, though, we can say that the term refers to the deployment of unusual (rare, experimental, expensive, non-standard) technologies or treatment regimes, or of ordinary technologies or treatment regimes beyond their usual limits.

Most of the examples ordinarily offered concern care for the terminally ill—a heart–lung machine being hooked up to someone who is (virtually) brain-dead, and so on. Such cases constitute poor paradigms, though. Philosophically, special and especially difficult complications are posed by cases concerning the proper treatment of people who would otherwise (and who may, anyway) cease to be.

Those may constitute the limiting cases of heroic treatments. Here, however, I shall focus on other kinds of cases where such complications are absent. Among these are extraordinary measures for creating life (*in vitro* fertilization and suchlike) and extraordinary measures for improving the quality of the lives of the handicapped (e.g. the electrical stimulation of paraplegics' muscles to simulate walking[1]). The conclusions that I reach in analysing those cases may be applied, *mutatis mutandis*, to the dying—although exactly what the '*mutatis mutandis*' clause might require in that very special case may well prove to be enormously difficult question.

What I shall be doing here is offering considerations that militate against deployment of such heroic measures. I do not presume that these considerations will always prove conclusive: far from it. But in the delicate balancing that is always required in the sort of desperate circumstances that characteristically occasion heroic measures, these considerations should always at least be weighed. And they may well, from time to time—and, in certain classes of cases, may even characteristically—tip that balance.

I

It seems distinctly odd to be arguing against heroic measures. Heroism is something we ordinarily regard as *exceptionally good*. But the term

[1] I have in mind here the sorts of experiments reported in *Time* 13 December 1982.

'exceptionally' good is telling. From the point of view of the person performing the acts of heroism, such acts are exceptional in the sense of being above and beyond the call of duty—where, as on Urmson's analysis, the limits of duty are set at what can reasonably be expected of competent moral agents.[2] Correlatively, from the point of view of the beneficiary of heroic interventions, such acts are also exceptional in the sense of being rare events, since 'what can reasonably be expected' evokes (for moralists, as for lawyers) a sense of the 'normal' that has a certain frequentist tinge about it.

The sense of the 'heroic' that is carried over from this standard analysis of heroism into the analysis of heroic therapeutic interventions retains an air of the extraordinary and the exceptional. But in that application, the notion of the 'heroic' is broadened somewhat.

There are, in fact, two senses in which medical treatment might qualify as 'heroic measures'. The first is the same sense as that in which heroes themselves are rare: i.e. the requisite performances are made only occasionally. A second sense in which medical treatments might qualify as 'heroic' is that it is only the exceptional patient who will, if given the treatment, actually derive any benefit from it. One in a hundred, or one in a thousand patients might benefit from some experimental cancer cure if it were administered equally to all of them, suppose. That, too, would count as a 'heroic' form of treatment.

Whichever the sense in which the treatment is heroic or exceptional, however, it is always presumed to be exceptionally good. It is that presumption of goodness which I next turn to query.

II

Heroic measures are presumed always to be good: certainly, at least from the point of view of the recipient; and by virture of that, at least presumptively from the point of view of society at large. Think of the case of the terminally ill. Without the heroic treatment, they would cease to live. Assuming that the treatment in view promises (with *whatever* probability, however small) a life that is worth living for them, then it is at least from their point of view better that they should receive the treatment than not. Any chance of a good life is better than no chance of a good life.

There is nothing special about the terminally ill in this regard. The same easy presumption of the desirability of heroic measures can be grounded on the same sort of logic for those who are not terminally ill.

[2] J. O. Urmson, 'Saints and Heroes', *Essays in Moral Philosophy*, A. I. Melden (ed.) (Seattle: University of Washington Press, 1958), 198–216.

Suppose the paraplegic's life is worth living; it is not as rich or varied as that of the able-bodied, perhaps, but it is better than nothing. Still, a life with some mobility is, presumably, better than a life spent entirely in a wheelchair; and any chance of a better life is better than no chance of a better life. So heroic measures to enable the cripple to 'walk' are presumably good, just so long as the treatment does not entail any downside risk of something even worse than the cripple's present paraplegia (e.g. quadraplegia).

In practice, of course, heroic measures sometimes do offer precisely that: a lottery that has, as its possible outcomes, either a life that is very much better than the one presently being enjoyed or one that is very much worse.[3] In cases such as that, heroic measures are neither presumptively good nor presumptively bad. To decide whether they are good or bad, in any particular case of this sort, we must consider the relevant probabilities, the values attached to each possible outcome, and the value or disvalue associated with risk-taking *per se*.

Those, however, are considerations that I would like to bracket out for purposes of this discussion. For present purposes, let us suppose that heroic measures pose no downside risk whatsoever. In what follows, I shall be supposing that heroic measures will either make the recipients of such treatments better off or else they will leave them no worse off than they would have been in the absence of the treatment.

III

Even after all that has been bracketed out, there still is, I shall argue, a sense in which heroic measures in medicine may leave their recipients worse off. This is through engendering 'false hopes'.[4] It may be good (albeit above and beyond the call of duty) for us to be heroes. But it is wrong for others to expect heroic performances from us; and it is wrong for us to lead people on in this respect, causing them to expect more heroism than is actually afoot. If the expectation follows inevitably from the performance, then that is an argument against the performance itself. Such is the structure of my argument here.

Heroic measures have been described above as 'unusual'. They are heroic either because they are not often undertaken, or else because

---

[3] In discussion of 'death with dignity', perhaps this is precisely what is at issue: living like *that* is worse than not living at all.

[4] My argument against holding out hopes of heroic medical interventions thus parallels arguments against holding out hopes of miracles: even if miraculous cures do sometimes happen, we do a disservice to those who are afflicted to hold out any real hope that each of them will be cured in this way.

Robert E. Goodin

they do not often work to produce the desired effects. In medical applications, especially, these two aspects of heroism are often connected: measures that usually do no good are not usually undertaken, precisely because usually they would not work anyway.[5] Certainly not all cases fit that mould, and I shall return later to discuss cases where failure to undertake heroic measures cannot be thus justified. For now, however, let us focus upon cases where that analysis is accurate. For those cases, at least, we may legitimately equate 'heroic measures' with 'low-probability-of-success treatments'.

In analysing what might be wrong about offering people low-probability treatments, it is important to recall that people are *offered* such treatments. People are not forced to accept such treatments; they are not given the treatments unless they, or someone acting as their agent, consent to it. Now, we regularly let people take risks. Some of them carry a very real possibility of undesirable outcomes; some of those undesirable outcomes entail serious damage to their health or other vital interests. Still, we are perfectly comfortable in letting people engage in those risky ventures, just so long as we are sure that certain basic preconditions are met (their consent is present, it is fully voluntary, well-informed, reflects their settled preferences, etc.). Why, then should we have any qualms about letting people take risks (even very bad—i.e. low-probability—ones) of *improving* their health, especially where *ex hypothesi* the treatment could *only* improve their health and never worsen it? That, on its face, seems to present something of a puzzle.

My resolution of that puzzle will focus on the role that offering people low-probability treatments plays in engendering in them (or those who care about them) false hopes, and on the way that such false hopes in turn undermine people's welfare.

IV

Before turning to my own argument as to why this is true, let me distinguish mine from a more familiar method of arguing for similar conclusions. It is well known that people's probability judgments are subject to all sorts of unwarranted influences. Building on those familiar propositions, it might be thought that what is wrong with heroic medical interventions is that they lead people to imagine that the probability of success is far higher than it actually is.

[5] 'Standard practice' is defined in that way, at least for purposes of defining malpractice and medical negligence—see George P. Fletcher, 'Legal Aspects of the Decision Not to Prolong Life', *Journal of the American Medical Association* **203** (1968), 65–68.

The phenomenon on view here is that of 'wishful thinking'. The people we are talking about here are in need of medical assistance; no treatment is particularly promising, so we have to resort to long shots. In such circumstances, proposing to people certain 'heroic' measures activates within them a well-known psychological mechanism whereby the wish, rather than the evidence, becomes the father to the belief. They very much hope that the heroic measure will work; and, hoping that it will, they come to believe that it will.[6]

This is to say that the problem with false hopes engendered by heroic medical treatments lies in the false beliefs people have about their probability of success. Desperate people will just not believe that the probabilities of success of the treatment are as low as they have every reason to believe that they are. Or, even if in some sense they cognitively accept the proposition, they will not be able to bring themselves to act upon it. Their actions, and perhaps their beliefs as well, will be irrational in this respect.[7]

Two special features of the case of heroic medical interventions make this particularly plausible. More straightforwardly, such treatments are typically offered only to people who are desperate; and desperate people are known for clutching at straws. Less straightforwardly, but perhaps just as importantly, there is a large body of psychometric evidence that people have trouble assimilating and acting rationally upon propositions about low-probability events. They employ a variety of heuristics—wholly unjustifiable, on any statistical grounds—that lead them to overweigh some probabilities and underweigh others in their decisions.[8] Perhaps the most important such mental shortcut in the present context is the so-called 'availability heuristic'. The dramatic being more memorable than the mundane, people tend to overestimate the probability of the former events relative to that of the latter. Thus, people overestimate the probability of dying from snakebite, and underestimate the probability of dying from heart attacks. By the same token, perhaps, patients offered low-probability treatments will seize upon the rare successes as the more 'available' (i.e. more memorable) mental model, and overestimate the frequence of miraculous cures relative to that of mundane failures. Either way—or both ways—people

[6] Bernard Williams, 'Deciding to Believe', *Problems of the Self* (Cambridge University Press, 1973), 136–151, David Pears, *Motivated Irrationality* (Oxford: Clarendon Press, 1984).

[7] Sometimes, of course, hope is itself therapeutic, i.e. a patient's belief in the likely success of the treatment causes it to succeed. There, it is not only pragmatically but epistemically rational to believe the treatment will succeed, for believing will make it so.

[8] Daniel Kahneman, Paul Slovic and Amos Tversky (eds), *Judgment Under Uncertainty* (Cambridge University Press, 1982).

are likely to have false beliefs regarding the probability of success of heroic medical interventions.

But mis-estimating frequencies or probabilities, in and of itself, does not always matter. Usually, false beliefs have harmful consequences—at least on average, over the long haul, etc.[9] In the circumstances here envisaged, however, it is hard to see how they can. *Ex hypothesi*, the treatment in view can only make people better off than they would otherwise have been or leave them in precisely the same state as they would otherwise have been. 'Otherwise have been' should be understood to embrace the alternative courses of treatment that they might have undertaken, as well as the course that the disease would have taken if left untreated.[10]

The upshot of those assumptions made for the purposes of the present argument is that pursuing the long-shot strategy is a 'strictly dominant' strategy. That is, it is no worse than any other strategy one might pursue in any possible state of the world, and it is better than any other strategy in at least some possible state of the world. Where a strictly dominant strategy of this sort is available, it is a uniquely rational course to pursue. For that judgment to be true, it does not matter *how* dominant it is—how many states of the world there are in which it is actually better rather than merely at least as good as other strategies, or how likely those preferred states of the world are to occur. And since probabilities are of no consequence in cases of strictly dominant strategies, neither are false beliefs about probabilities.

In short, the penalty that we ordinarily pay for acting in reliance on false beliefs about probabilities is here waived. That is true by virtue of the assumption that heroic medical interventions can only make the recipient better off than he would otherwise have been or leave him exactly as he would otherwise have been. While that assumption is not always warranted, the most interesting cases of heroic interventions occur when it is; and I shall for the purposes of the present exercise persist in focusing upon those cases exclusively.

V

In the previous argument, harm was done to people by their beliefs that the probability that heroic measures would succeed was higher than it

[9] This is formalized in, e.g., George A. Akerlof and William T. Dickens, 'The Economic Consequences of Cognitive Dissonance', *American Economic Review* **72** (1982), 305–319.

[10] It would hardly have been good practice for doctors to have offered a low-probability treatment where there was some higher-probability one available; and the aim of this paper is to discover what might be said against even 'good medical practice' in this regard, rather than merely to score easy points indicting bad practice.

actually was. The fatal flaw in that argument was that that turns out not to be a harm at all, because in the circumstances here postulated people's choices are unaffected by their probability judgments, distorted or otherwise. The harm that I shall next be considering derives simply from holding out any hope at all to desperate people. When we propose to someone some heroic measure or another to alleviate the problem, we are thereby holding out some hope—some possibility—of success. That in itself harms people I shall now argue. The harm that comes to people, on this argument, derives from the distortion in their life plans that is produced by the introduction of successful treatment even as a mere possibility. That, rather than any exaggerated notions they may harbour as to its chances of success, is the real source of their injury.

What is wrong with false hopes is that they lead people to pursue illusory goals. Those goals are illusory, first, because they are (probably) unattainable. That, in turn, makes them illusory in a second sense as well. The very goodness of the goal is itself an illusion; and that is true for reasons connected, somehow, to the unattainability of the goal. It turns out to be not merely foolish but positively harmful, in some way or another, to pursue goals that are unattainable.

There are basically two ways of going about analysing what is wrong with (probably) unattainable goals. One appeals to standards that are external to the agent himself; the other appeals to standards that are somehow internal to the agent himself. Appeal to external standards would be more powerful, if only those standards could somehow be validated. But that, of course, is a tricky business. Internal standards are less contentious and, motivationally at least, no less compelling. The bulk of my argument will therefore be couched in those terms, after only a brief nod in the direction of the sorts of external standards which might be employed in this connection.

The external standard to which arguments against false hopes might appeal is just a variation on the classic stoical argument that people should (for the sake of their own happiness, or peace of mind) revise their desires in light of what they can realistically expect to get. This principle requires only a little revision in the present context. The point of the stoics is couched in terms of possibilities: people ought not desire that which is impossible. What is at issue with heroic therapeutic interventions is improbable, not impossible, goals. But the basic stoic point retains its force there, too: people will only make themselves miserable pursuing goals that are probably beyond their reach, or devoting more effort (or attaching greater hopes) to goals than their objective probabilities of attainment truly warrant.

(Although I have called this an appeal to 'external' standards, it is worth noting that even the stoics appeal to certain internal features of a person's own preferences. They say that a person would be happier if he were to forsake the pursuit of impossible goals: that is why he should forsake them. But in that case, it is the person's own preference to pursue goals that are possible that is producing the results; it is not some external standard saying that it is good for him to restrict himself in this way, whether he wants to do so or not. I say this not in criticism of the stoic argument on this point, which I find perfectly sensible, but rather in criticism of the supposition that we can get very far with a genuinely external standard in these areas at all.)

Whether or not we can appeal to external standards for these purposes, it is clear that we can make a very powerful appeal indeed to internal standards. And this strong sort of internal appeal must be distinguished from the relatively weak form of appeal that addresses only those who explicitly want to be realistic from the start. Some people do, others do not. Any argument that is hinged on brute facts about people's first-order preferences in this way would be powerfully compromised by their variable first-order preferences in this matter.

The more powerful form of internal appeal turns instead upon reasons people have for regarding heroic measures as *prima facie* undesirable, whether or not they actually do. These are reasons that are still, in some sense, internal to people's own existing preferences. But they are reasons that lie beneath the surface level of their first-order preference themselves.[11]

The key to this argument is just this. Life plans are complex things with various interactions between the particular projects that comprise them. Heroic interventions, if successful, would make a big difference to those plans.[12] Their success would require a comprehensive revision

---

[11] Another way of finding preferences for realistic preferences implicit in people's first-order preferences seems less promising. We might point to the undeniable psychological fact that people generally adapt to circumstances: if it is clear that they cannot have something, they usually come not to want it, or at least not to pine for it; they resign themselves perfectly well, if not perfectly happily, to doing without it. But we cannot infer from this that people have a meta-preference to learn to do without the therapy in view, for while the cure is improbable it is not impossible. In these circumstances the psychological tendency toward wishful thinking has as much claim to represent people's deeper preference ordering as does the psychological tendency to resign oneself to one's fate.

[12] We would not call them 'heroic' if they did not. But semantics aside, we would have no grounds for taking an action with such low chances of success unless the change it might make would be substantial. All heroic measures make a big difference, but not all that makes a big difference is necessarily 'heroic', in the sense of being rare or unusual. Hay fever injections for serious

of those plans, not just some marginal adjustments. If a cripple could walk, his life would change completely; if a childless couple had children, their lives would change completely; and so on.

Thus, people with the prospect of heroic interventions find themselves at a fork in their lives. Depending on how things turn out, they will want to pursue very different life plans. These are typically incompatible alternatives: they must pursue either one or the other, and cannot hedge their bets by pursuing a little of both. And typically choices between such alternatives are substantially irreversible: once having set out down one path, it is costly if not impossible to go back to the fork again and start out down the other instead.[13] In any case, even where hedging and backtracking might be possible, there is a good reason to avoid it: a life of equivocation and false starts is a less good life than is one characterized by more coherence and consistency.[14]

The upshot is that people facing the prospect of a heroic intervention must hold all their other plans in abeyance pending the outcome of

---

sufferers might be an example. The objections here lodged against heroic measures are usually waived in the case of such non-heroic measures precisely because, being not uncommon, they usually do not interrupt people's life plans in the same way as heroic measures do. But if it should happen that, despite their being not uncommon, these non-heroic measures nonetheless did somehow cause people to get stuck at a fork in their lives, then the same objections would apply.

[13] Economists appreciate that, in an uncertain world, it is valuable to have options; and irreversible choices, because they foreclose options, carry a special penalty in those terms. See, e.g., Kenneth J. Arrow and Anthony C. Fisher, 'Environmental Preservation, Uncertainty and Irreversibility', *Quarterly Journal of Economics* **88** (1974), 312–319. Again, this penalty is not an infinitely large one, so it may well be right that we should often pursue irreversible courses of action despite this consideration that always militates against them. Of course, heroic measures themselves are often option-preserving strategies, on the part of doctors presented with, e.g., a comatose patient brought into the casualty ward; and once hooked up to life-preserving equipment, it may be hard to get a patient unhooked. But insofar as they can anticipate that the latter proposition is going to be true, doctors are wrong about the former position. That is, if they are going to be locked into continuing treatment, once started, then starting treatment forecloses options just as much as not starting it.

[14] Robert Nozick, *Philosophical Explanations* (Cambridge, Mass.: Harvard University Press, 1981), 403–450; Richard Wollheim, *The Thread of Life* (Cambridge University Press, 1984). Those arguments characteristically appeal, in the first instance, to external standards of 'the good', it is true. But those standards will prove sufficiently compelling in terms of a sufficiently large portion of possible life plans that most people will embrace them as internal standards for judging the success of their own lives, as well.

those interventions.[15] The final step in the argument against heroic measures is to say that that waiting is itself costly to people. It may entail actual out-of-pocket expenses. But at the very least, it will entail 'opportunity costs': there are various other projects that people could be pursuing, but are not pursuing, pending the outcome of the heroic intervention.

Of course, the price of waiting is a price that people would only too happily pay if the interventions turn out ultimately to succeed. My point is just that it *is* a price that people have to pay for heroic interventions, whether they succeed or fail.

The structure of my argument in section IV above, in replying to the probablistic form of criticism of heroic interventions, was to say that heroic interventions as here construed constitute no-lose propositions: either they leave you better off than you would otherwise have been or else they leave you exactly as you would otherwise have been.

The structure of my argument in this section is to say that, because that lottery is not played out instantaneously, heroic interventions constitute always-costly propositions: succeed or fail, they always entail interruption to your life choices pending their outcomes. How great those costs might be varies.[16] Whether those costs are worth paying varies. It is no part of my claim that heroic medical interventions are always, on net, disadvantageous.[17] My claim is merely that there are always these costs to be weighed in the balance.

[15] Their only alternatives are to proceed on the improbable assumption that the heroic measures will succeed (in which case they will face great costs in reversing those choices when they fail, if they can reverse them at all), or else to proceed on the more likely assumption that they will fail (in which case they will face great costs in reversing those choices should they succeed, if they can be reversed at all, and enormous regret at their choices if they cannot be reversed).

[16] It varies, among other things, with the time it takes for those uncertainties to play themselves out. If there is always 'one more possibility' just around the corner, then people's life choices may be suspended virtually indefinitely. If there are few possibilities and quick resolutions, the interference might be slight.

[17] That is to say, I see no grounds for supposing that the various factors bearing on this decision vary systematically with one another, in either direction. The only moderately plausible argument along these lines I can see for heroic interventions is to say that the less difference it will make to your life the less paralysing it will be on your future planning. But that is not to say that hedging and backtracking is more possible (or even less costly) in those cases; it is merely to say that it is less worthwhile there. The more nearly indifferent we are between the alternative paths before us, the less we mind irrevocably committing ourselves to one and forsaking the other forever.

(As I said at the outset of this paper, the terminally ill constitute a special case. Now we can see why. According to the conventional wisdom, anyway, the terminally ill can have no alternative plans to hold in abeyance pending the outcome of heroic interventions, and in this way are radically unlike others who might be offered such interventions: if the intervention fails the terminally ill die, whereas if IVF fails the couple carries on their very different life without children. Of course, this conventional wisdom misconstrues the situation of the terminally ill. They will typically want to make plans—euphemistically, to 'arrange their affairs'—even if it is only to die well. And in any case, the life choices of their families and friends will be held in abeyance pending the outcome of the terminally ill patient's treatment, even if he himself has no plans that are being held in abeyance. More generally, taking the terminally ill thus misconstrued as the paradigm case for heroic interventions quite wrongly implies that those offered heroic medical interventions typically have no choice—or at least no acceptable choice—but to hope that the long shot succeeds. Even as regards the terminally ill that is not true, as advocates of hospices and holistic medicine rightly argue against advocates of aggressive surgery. It is all the more untrue as regards childless couples or paraplegics, who really do have possibilities for perfectly reasonable lives even without heroic interventions.)

The argument developed so far constitutes a case for an individual's rejecting heroic measures in his own case, on the grounds that they entail costs in excess of their probable benefits.[18] But we can build on that proposition to come to a case for rejecting certain whole classes of heroic measures quite generally, as a matter of public policy rather than merely personal choice.

The bridging proposition required here is much like the psychological proposition developed in section IV above. Wishful thinking being what it is, people will, if offered the prospect of a heroic medical treatment, imagine that the treatment has a better chance of success than it really does. In consequence, they will weigh the probable benefits of the treatment too heavily, relative to its costs; and they will make what, by their own standards of value, is the objectively wrong

---

[18] More formally, heroic measures should be rejected if the opportunity costs of waiting to see how they turn out exceed the utility of success, discounted by its improbability, less the utility of the best alternative life available absent the heroic measure. Ideally, this is a calculation that rational individuals should perform for themselves, in deciding whether to seek or forswear heroic measures. But the well-established psychological dynamic of 'responsibility avoidance' may prevent them from acting rationally in this regard, and thus constitute yet another reason for public policies against heroic measures (see Kahneman, Slovic and Tversky, op. cit., for the psychometric evidence).

27

choice. In section IV, their mis-estimates of probabilities did not matter, because heroic measures were seen as costless. Having here come to see how errors of this sort can be costly, making mistakes about probabilities can indeed cause harm. Here, there is a very real penalty to be paid from making the wrong choice, and that is what mistaken probability assessments trick people into doing.

Roughly speaking, the broad classes of heroic medical interventions that might be less attractive in that light would be ones displaying either (or both) of the following characteristics. One is that the ultimate outcome of the treatment regime will not become apparent for quite some time. The other is that those who would receive the treatments would have reasonly good alternative life choices available to them, even in the absence of the treatment.[19] The former consideration speaks to questions of costs of holding other plans in abeyance for a very long time while the consequences of the treatment play themselves out; the latter speaks to questions of benefits of the treatment regime, compared to those that would be realized even if that treatment were withheld. The higher the costs or the lower the benefits of a treatment regime characteristically are, the more wary we ought to be of offering it to people at all.[20]

VI

None of this constitutes an ironclad argument against heroic medical interventions, either in general or as applied to particular treatments or

---

[19] 'Good life choices available to them' is intentionally equivocal, as between our objective and their subjective assessment of those options. There is a case, in terms of efficiency, for allocating scarce or heroic treatments to paraplegics who simply refuse to reconcile themselves to life in a wheelchair as a subjectively unacceptable alternative. But that is inequitable, in the sense of penalizing the virtuous who come to terms with their condition; and we may, for that reason, prefer to make policy on the basis of an objective assessment of how well off people are rather than responding to their subjective assessments.

[20] Also involved in such calculations is the consideration of just how much of an interruption to people's lives the prospect of heroic treatment might be. If they can get on with a large part of their lives, even pending resolution of the uncertainty—or if they can make contingent plans for the future, depending upon how it turns out, that do not have to be implemented until after the uncertainty has played itself out—then the costs would once again be cancelled. The two conditions in the text are more appropriate to the concerns of policymakers than this one, only because most of the people offered any given heroic intervention will usually find themselves in much the same position with respect to those matters, whereas this third consideration is much more contingent upon the particulars of each person's own life plan.

particular patients. At most, I can only claim to have shown that there is always a price to be paid for such interventions, and that there ought therefore to be a presumption against rather than in favour of such interventions. But this presumption, like all presumptions, is eminently rebuttable. Any given person may suppose the price worth paying. And say what we will about the general propensity among people toward wishful thinking, any given individual may be seeing matters perfectly clearly in so judging.

All that to one side, however, there is yet another way in which heroic medical interventions might be justified, notwithstanding all the arguments lodged against them above. Suppose that heroic measures involve treatments with a low probability of success, as suggested above. But further suppose that the probabilities of success improve with each successive trial; i.e. doctors learn from their experience. And suppose, finally, that that is the only way that the doctors can learn what they need to know in order to perfect the treatment.

The heroic medical interventions might be justified in roughly the same way that we justify using the terminally ill as subjects for trials of long-shot cancer cures. Someone has to be the guinea-pig. Giving these patients the treatment engenders in them false hopes; but someone has to be given false hopes in order that subsequent patients can have a real hope.

We are naturally—and quite rightly—queasy about using the terminally ill in these ways, necessary though that may be. We build in various safeguards, and impose various conditions, before this can be done to them. Surely we ought to hedge heroic medical interventions, thus rationalized, with similar constraints?[21] Perhaps the most central of these, for present purposes, is the requirement that we have *some* reason (analogous to promising results from animal experiments, in the case of cancer cures) for supposing that the heroic intervention might do some good, even for the present patients who are basically acting as guinea-pigs. That is just to say, it may be an unfortunate necessity to engender in people largely false hopes, but it is never permissible to engender in them hopes that are *entirely* false.

---

[21] 'Informed consent' is certainly among them—though here, as with many medical experiments, informing people that the treatment probably will not work may well compromise the success of the experiment. Just as a scientifically sound drug trial may require giving people in a control group placebos without telling them, so too might we have scientific grounds for withholding information about the realistic chances of success with heroic interventions. How these scientific considerations are traded off for ethical ones is, of course, a notoriously difficult problem. It is not, however, one unique to the cases I am here considering.

Furthermore, the arguments of this essay militate against the premature reporting of the results of such experiments to the public at large. The tabloids often carry reports of some new 'miracle' cure for some deadly disease. Upon closer inspection, it often turns out that these cures are a very long way off, still. Such announcements often come just as the cures have been approved for some very preliminary stage of (e.g. rodent) testing; anyone currently suffering the condition they purport to cure will be long dead before the cure is approved, even on an experimental basis, for human use. Such reporting is simply irresponsible, raising the hopes of readers suffering from such conditions utterly without justification. So my arguments about the costs of engendering false hopes have implications for the reporting as well as the conduct of these sorts of experiments.

VII

In any case, this experimentalist rationale for heroic interventions cannot justify all such activities. Often the probabilities do not get better in successive trials, and cannot be expected to do so. This is especially true if the low probability reflects something analogous to what I have called the 'lack of heroes' in section I above, rather than merely the inefficacy of heroic efforts. Suppose the reason that a treatment regime has a low probability of success derives from the fact that it is a style of treatment that is grossly underfunded within the health service as a whole. Assuming that the more we have already spent the less we are now prepared to spend on the treatment, one heroic intervention reduces the funding (and hence probability of success) of the next. So, assuming subsequent interventions are not that much cheaper than the first, any one heroic intervention in this case would undermine rather than assist treatment of similar cases in future. That is not, of course, to say that they should not be undertaken; it is only to say that they cannot be justified on this pump-priming logic.

From this, a further implication follows: if the health service goes in for heroic measures, it should buy enough to go around to everyone similarly situated. The logic of this proposition is simple. If one person has been given a certain treatment, then anyone else suffering the same condition might reasonably regard it as being at least *possible* that he will be given the same treatment. Heroic measures for one person in this way create, if not exactly an expectation, at least a hope of similar treatment among all others in the same condition. Those hopes, insofar as they are false (meaning, in this context, insofar as treatment will not be forthcoming) entail costs of the sort that I have here been discussing.

Heroic treatments are costly, too, of course. Which cost should, in any given case, predominate in the social calculus is an open question. I am perfectly prepared to believe that, at some point well before everyone in need has been treated, we may rightly decide that incurring the cost of false hopes is to be preferred to increasingly costly treatment of patients with increasingly unpromising prognoses. Still, here again, the costs of engendering false hopes always have to be weighed in the balance. This serves as one more consideration arguing in favour of a more rather than less generous funding for the health services, and for a more rather than less equal distribution of such benefits as they can afford to provide.

If we have decided that heroic measures are to be undertaken on behalf of less than the whole population that might benefit from them, then at the very least we ought to be frank about how many people we are prepared to treat in this way. That, in turn, has implications for how many people ought to be allowed to join the queue for treatment. If it is clear (whether as a matter of policy, or for any other reason) that we will be able to perform only ten heart–lung transplants per year, for the foreseeable future, then it is simply irresponsible to let several hundred people join the queue for such treatment. By allowing them to join the queue at all, we hold out to them some possibility of treatment, even if by telling most of them that they are far down the queue we indicate that the probability of their being treated is slight. The mere possibility of treatment engenders false hopes, with the costs that I have here been discussing.

Notice, finally, that it is the *promise* of treatment, rather than treatment *per se*, that generates false hopes. The paraplegic hopes that technology will soon develop to enable him to walk. The IVF patient hopes that it works next time. And so on.

Some heroic medical interventions entail such promises for the future. Others do not. Imagine the case of a stagnant technology, with no prospect in either the short or even medium term of any breakthroughs. Suppose further that a single application of this 'heroic' technology will decisively determine the results that any given patient might expect from it; if it does not work the first time, there is no point trying it another time. Suppose further that all patients who could possibly benefit from such treatment are given it immediately upon being identified, so there is no waiting involved. *Then* application of these 'heroic' technologies would resolve uncertainties rather than engendering them, and would be immune to the criticisms lodged against them in section V above.

Needless to say, most technologies are not like that. In the real world there are—and probably always will be—queues. With most treatments, no single trial is conclusive for any given case—if only because the medics might have misapplied the technology or misread the results. And most technologies develop in unpredictable ways at unpredictable rates—we can never be sure that the technology is stagnant, and useless for a person in the future if it is proven to be useless for him now.

With respect to queues and mistakes, we might be inclined to express the pious hope that they be eliminated. If they are, those objectives to this strategy for rescuing heroic medical interventions from the criticisms here lodged against them would drop away. But no one can wish an end to breakthroughs in technologies that enhance the quality of people's lives. So even in the real world, some of my criticisms of heroic medical interventions for raising false hopes will retain their force.

Again, nothing I have said should be taken as a conclusive argument against medical innovation. My argument is merely that there is always a price to be paid, in terms of the false hopes it engenders and the harm that they do to people. But that may be a price that we should be prepared to pay.[22]

[22] I am grateful to audiences at the Universities of Stockholm and York for comments on earlier versions of this essay.

Quality of Life and Resource Allocation

MICHAEL LOCKWOOD

A new word has recently entered the British medical vocabulary. What it stands for is neither a disease nor a cure. At least, it is not a cure for a disease in the medical sense. But it could, perhaps, be thought of as an intended cure for a medicosociological disease: namely that of haphazard or otherwise ethically inappropriate allocation of scarce medical resources. What I have in mind is the term 'QALY', which is an acronym standing for *quality adjusted life year.* Just what this means and what it is intended to do I shall explain in due course. Let me first, however, set the scene.

I

Problems of resource allocation within medicine arise at a number of different levels. First, one might ask how much of a society's resources should be devoted to health care at all, as opposed to housing, say, or defence. (For what it may be worth, the United States is usually said to devote 10 per cent of its gross national product to health care—though some authors claim that the true figure is substantially higher. By contrast, most Western European countries devote about 7 or 8 per cent, whereas Britain devotes only 5.6 per cent. It is widely held, however, that Britain's relatively low figure is largely compensated for by substantially greater cost efficiency, as compared with other countries. Perhaps; certainly this argument is regularly paraded by the British Government whenever it is suggested that the National Health Service is underfunded!) Given some overall allocation of resources to health care in general, one can then ask how these resources should be distributed amongst various different sorts of health care expenditure: for example, primary versus hospital care, or preventive medicine versus care of the already ill. Then, within such broader categories, one can ask how one should distribute between different specializations: cardiac versus obstetric units, say, in the case of hospital medicine. And both within and across specializations, one can ask what should be the relative funds allocated for different forms of treatment: kidney transplants versus renal dialysis, hip replacement operations versus coronary by-pass surgery, cervical smears versus primary geriatric nursing care.

Michael Lockwood

It is customary to lump together questions of all these different sorts as problems of *macroallocation*. *Micro*allocation questions, by contrast, arise when decisions have already been made about matters of the kinds just instanced. One has, let us suppose, more patients who stand to benefit by a certain form of treatment than it is possible, given limited resources, to give the treatment to. And the question is: who then gets it? What sorts of criteria should one then appeal to? What selection procedures should one adopt? This problem assumes a special poignancy, of course, when the treatment in question is one without which patients will die. The dramatic potential of such decisions has been widely exploited in fiction, from Bernard Shaw's *The Doctor's Dilemma* (1911)[1] to James Balfour's (1969) short story 'The Junior Physician and the Court of Final Appeal'[2] and a 1966 *Dr Kildare* series, in which a lay panel is established by Dr Gillespie to decide which of a number of clinically eligible patients should be chosen for a limited number of places on a newly installed artificial kidney machine. (The model for Dr Gillespie's committee appears to have been the so-called 'God Committee' of the Seattle Artificial Kidney Center, which from 1961 to 1967 sat in judgment over patients suffering from end-stage renal failure).[3]

Now a natural response to allocation problems, both at macro and micro levels, is to say simply: one should put one's resources where they will do the most good. Well, yes, perhaps one should. But that then raises the further question: what does one mean by 'the most good'? One kind of good, arguably the most important kind of good, that health care may achieve is the saving of lives, or more precisely (if less optimistically) postponing death. So one measure—albeit a very crude and one-sided measure—of the good that health care does would be the overall extension of live expectancy that it generates: years of life gained. Some writers have argued that we should give a very high priority to this aim of maximizing aggregate years of life gained; and that, moreover, this aim morally requires an allocation of resources, both within and outside medicine, that is radically at odds with the present allocation pattern in developed countries. So argued Dr Donald Gould in 1975:

> In the name of justice, as well as efficiency, we have got to adopt new methods of medical accounting. One such assesses the relative

---

[1] Bernard Shaw, *The Doctor's Dilemma: A Tragedy* (first published in 1911), A. C. Ward (ed.) (London: Longman's Green, 1960).

[2] 'The Junior Physician and the Court of Last Appeal', in James Balfour, *Court Short* (London: Hutchinson, 1969), 171–189.

[3] Guido Calebresi and Philip Bobbit, *Tragic Choices* (New York: W. W. Norton, 1978), 187–188, 209 n., 232–233 n.

importance of threats to health in terms of the loss of life-years they cause. Calculations are based upon the assumption that all who survive their first perilous year ought then to live on to the age of 70 (any extra years are a bonus). In Denmark, for example, there are 50,000 deaths a year, but only 20,000 among citizens in the 1–70 bracket. These are the ones that count. The annual number of life-years lost in this group totals 264,000. Of these, 80,000 are lost because of accidents and suicides, 40,000 because of coronary heart disease, and 20,000 are due to lung disease. On the basis of these figures, a large proportion of the 'health' budget ought to be spent on preventing accidents and suicides and a lesser but still substantial amount on attempting to prevent and cure heart and lung disease. Much less would be spent on cancer, which is predominantly a disease of the latter half of life, and which therefore contributes relatively little to the total sum of life-years lost. Little would go towards providing kidney machines, and even less towards treating haemophiliacs. No money at all would be available for trying to prolong the life of a sick old man of 82.[4]

There are several things that might be said in response to this passage. First, it is unclear why Gould thinks that *justice,* as well as efficiency, calls for these methods of medical accounting. What is involved in being just, in such contexts, is a question to which we shall return in due course. Secondly, Gould is here concentrating on quantity of life lived to the exclusion of its quality. Most of what is done in the name of health care is directed towards the alleviation of pain, discomfort and disability, rather than the extension of life, but is surely no less valuable on that account. Moreover, things which rank equal in terms of the threat to life that they pose, may well rank unequal in terms of their effect on the quality of life, or in terms of the typical quality of the lives that they threaten to cut short; both sorts of consideration are surely relevant to the question of the relative priority to be given to their prevention or cure.

Thus, judgments about which of several forms of health care expenditure does the most good calls, in general, for one to balance against each other the life-enhancing and the life-extending aspects of health care: quality and quantity of life have somehow to be rendered mutually commensurable. This is where QALYs come in. I quote from Alan Williams, of the University of York, who has done most to develop this approach:

---

[4] Donald Gould, 'Some Lives Cost Too Dear', *New Statesman* November (1975), quoted in Jonathan Glover, *Causing Death and Saving Lives* (Harmondsworth: Penguin Books, 1977), 220–221.

The essence of a QALY is that it takes a year of healthy life expectancy to be worth 1, but regards a year of unhealthy life expectancy as worth less than 1. Its precise value is lower the worse the quality of life of the unhealthy person (which is what the 'quality adjusted' bit is all about). If being dead is worth zero, it is, in principle, possible for a QALY to be negative, i.e. for the quality of someone's life to be judged worse than being dead.

The general idea is that a beneficial health care activity is one that generates a positive amount of QALYs, and that an efficient health care activity is one where the cost per QALY is as low as it can be. A high priority health care activity is one where the cost-per-QALY is low, and a low priority activity is one where cost-per-QALY is high.[5]

The assumption here is that there is some rational way of trading off length of life against quality of life, so that one could say, for example, that three years of life with some specified degree of discomfort, loss of mobility or whatever was worth two years of normal life. Such trade-offs are, of course, often inescapable in medical practice. Take, for example, a patient suffering from laryngial carcinoma, where the choice of treatments is between laryngectomy, which is incompatible with normal speech, but has a 60 per cent five-year survival rate, and radiotherapy, which preserves normal speech but has only a 30–40 per cent five-year survival rate. Here, presumably, the ethically appropriate thing for the doctor to do is put the choice to the patient—both on the grounds of autonomy and on the grounds that the patient is probably better able to judge, in terms of his own values and way of life, what sort of impact on the quality of his own life the inability to speak normally is likely to have. (For what it is worth, nearly all patients, faced with this particular choice, in fact opt for surgery.) But the resource of passing the decision back to the individual patient is unavailable in microallocation cases, where different patients are competing for the same resource, and would both choose to be treated, or in macroallocation cases, where again we are dealing with different patients, this time mainly future patients, and with questions of overall funding.

What economists who favour the QALY approach do, in a macroallocation context, is take a checklist of health factors that are likely to affect the perceived quality of life of normal people, and assign weightings to them. (Most work done in Britain has been based on the *Rosser distress and disability index,* which health economists would be the first to admit provides only rather a crude measure of quality, but one

[5] Alan Williams, 'The Value of QALYs', *Health and Social Service Journal* July (1985), 3.

which they would hope to improve upon in time.[6]) There is, of course, an inescapable element of arbitrariness here, both in the choice of factors to be taken into account and in the relative weightings that are attached to them, which, as already pointed out, would differ markedly from patient to patient. (Immobility, for example, is likely to prove far more irksome to the athlete than to the philosopher.) But the factors and their associated weightings are mostly so chosen as to reflect the feelings and considered judgments which the average or representative patient is likely to evince in practice, when faced with various forms of disability or discomfort, either in prospect or, better, having actually experienced them. On this basis, a given form of treatment is assigned a QALY value, corresponding to the number of QALYs such a patient can look forward to with the treatment minus the number of QALYs the patient can look forward to if untreated. One then calculates what each QALY gained by these means actually costs.

Whatever philosophical reservations one might have about such an exercise (and I will turn to these in due course), it has yielded some interesting, indeed surprising, results. In Britain there is (or certainly was in the recent past) a widespread feeling that heart transplants represent a wasteful use of medical resources, that the benefits yielded are simply not sufficiently great to justify the cost. But on the other hand, people who say this will usually argue that not enough funds are, in Britain, allocated to long-term renal dialysis. It is widely regarded as a scandal that a treatment that is so effective in extending life should not be made universally available. Williams, evaluating these and other forms of treatment using the notion of a QALY, has come to a very different conclusion. Williams assigns to heart transplantation a QALY value of 4.5 (the point, neglected by most critics of heart transplants, being that their effect, when successful, on the quality of life is dramatic), whereas home and hospital dialysis receive QALY values of 6 and 5 respectively (the neglected point here being that, for most people, long-term dialysis represents a considerable ordeal).[7] Nevertheless, dialysis, so far, comes out somewhat ahead of heart transplants. But now the cost per patient of long-term dialysis is considerably greater than that of a heart transplant. So the cost per QALY is only £5,000 in the case of heart transplants, as compared to £11,000 and £14,000 respectively, in the case of home and hospital dialysis.[8]

[6] P. Kind, R. Rosser and A. Williams, 'Valuation of quality of life: Some Psychometric Evidence', in M. W. Jones-Lee, *The Value of Life and Safety* (Amsterdam: Elsevier/North-Holland, 1982).

[7] Alan Williams, 'Economics of Coronary Bypass Grafting', *British Medical Journal* **291** (3 August 1985), 328.

[8] Ibid.

Actually, all three figures turned out to be very high as compared with, say, hip replacement or heart valve replacement and pacemaker implantation, whereas Williams assesses the costs per QALY gained as, respectively, £750, £900 and £700;[9] in these latter operations one gets far more QALYs for one's money. In most parts of Britain there are waiting lists for all these operations; in the case of hip replacement operations the average waiting list under the National Health Service is three years (and in some areas is as high as five years)—it is not in the least unusual for people to die before they reach the head of the queue! Someone who believed that macroallocation in health care should be determined wholly on the basis of directing funds to where they can generate the maximum number of QALYs might well conclude from these figures that given a fixed health care budget, it would be rationally appropriate actually to transfer funds from such relatively high cost-per-QALY, albeit life-saving, forms of treatment as renal dialysis, to such things as hip-replacement operations, right up to the point at which the waiting lists had been eliminated—even if this meant providing no long-term dialysis at all! A pretty startling conclusion, hardly less radical than Gould's.

II

Appealing to QALYs in a macroallocation context, despite the fact that, as we have just seen, it is likely to result in recommendations wildly at odds with present practice, tends to raise fewer hackles than its application to problems of microallocation. Indeed, the advocates of this approach themselves tend to talk less about microallocation than macroallocation. But the approach has clear implications for micro-allocation too. It implies, for example, that life-saving treatment should, other things being equal, go to those who, with the treatment, will have a longer life expectancy; thus, generally speaking, it will favour younger over older patients. This is in line with actual policy within the British National Health Service with regard to renal dialysis: most centres operate an effective 65-year cut-off. It also implies that, if there appeared, on other grounds, to be nothing to choose between two rival candidates for some life-saving treatment, but one was suffering from a condition, whether or not related to whatever it was that threatened his life, that detracted from its quality, then one should prefer to treat the other candidate. These two sorts of consideration were run together in an example that became a bone of contention at the British Medical Association Annual Scientific Meeting at Oxford in April 1986.

[9] Ibid.

[S]ay two people needed lifesaving treatment and there were the resources to treat only one, say one was young and fit and the other was older with arthritis, who should get the treatment? If QALYs were used the younger patient would inevitably and always get the treatment but was that fair?[10]

The economist, Professor Alan Maynard, a champion of the QALY approach, defended such a policy; the philosopher John Harris attacked it, arguing that it was indefensibly discriminatory, and advocated instead the use of a lottery in such cases.

These health-care economists have, it appears, rediscovered utilitarianism. Indeed the QALY approach has a pleasantly nostalgic air, for those familiar with Jeremy Bentham's 'felicific calculus'.[11] Most of the philosophical doubts one might have about the QALY approach would be particular instances of familiar charges that have been laid against utilitarianism. It should be emphasized, however, that the use of QALYs does not commit one to *classical* or *eudaimonic* utilitarianism: that is to say, there is no suggestion that the good is to be equated with happiness. If we adopt a terminology recently advocated by Amartya Sen,[12] the QALY approach to allocation is, strictly speaking, *welfarist* rather than utilitarian—welfarism being the doctrine that we should so act as to maximize aggregate benefit. Classical utilitarianism is thus a particular form of welfarism, characterized by its equation of benefit with happiness. The concept of a QALY is, of course, committed to no such equation. Indeed, it is in one sense only a framework, requiring to be fleshed out by some substantive conception of what contributes to or detracts from the intrinsic value or worthwhileness of a life, and to what degree—a conception, that is, of what it is about a life that determines of how much benefit it is to the person whose life it is. To this extent, the concept is highly permissive: one can, as it were, plug in whatever conception of value one personally favours. The quality of life indices that are used in practice, as I indicated earlier, seem to be grounded in people's actual expressed values, preferences and attitudes. Is this because people are supposed, by and large, to be their own best judges of the degree to which various things do or would contribute to or detract from the value of their lives? Or is it because, whether they are the best judges or not, it is thought democratically proper that resource allocation reflect, as far as possible, people's actual

[10] Tessa Richards and Linda Beecham, 'The BMA in Oxford', *British Medical Journal* **292** (26 April 1986), 1119–1120.

[11] Jeremy Bentham, *The Principles of Morals and Legislation* (1789), Chs. 1–5.

[12] See Amartya Sen, 'Utilitarianism and Welfarism', *Journal of Philosophy* **76** (September 1979).

preferences—a kind of oblique appeal to personal autonomy? It is unclear, though it perhaps does not much matter for practical purposes. My own view is that there are actually three ways in which people's preferences are of moral relevance here. First, what people here and now want is something that ought to be given weight (though not necessarily decisive weight) in the name of a principle of collective or individual self-determination. Secondly, it is, other things being equal, in people's interests that their preferences are satisfied; to that extent the degree to which people's actual circumstances are consonant with their preferences is one of the things, but by no means the only thing, that should be taken into account in making an overall assessment of the quality of someone's life. And finally, people have what philosophers call 'privileged access' to their own lives; they know, better than anyone else can, just what it is like to be them. To that extent, their own judgments about conditions they have actually experienced, whilst far from infallible (especially where what it is that detracts from the quality of their lives is itself something that may affect their judgement, or, where relevant, memory), nevertheless have great authority.

Supposing that one were clear about *what* it was that one was trying to measure, there would still, of course, be room for considerable scepticism about the extent to which it was possible to measure it. From a certain point of view, the idea of putting a yardstick up against a life, whether real or hypothetical, and reading off some numerical value representing its quality or degree of worthwhileness, may seem simply preposterous. On the one hand, one might reasonably doubt whether the moral universe was so constituted that there was a fact of the matter as to just how many years of life under circumstances A were equivalent in value to one year of life under circumstances B, whether one were comparing within or across lives. And even assuming that there were uniquely correct answers to such questions, one might reasonably doubt whether there was any reliable method of divining them. (Interpersonal comparisons have, historically, been the subject of particular scepticism here, on both these grounds).

But one must be careful here. It would be a mistake to suppose that the validity or usefulness of the QALY approach hinged either on there being, or on one's being able to determine, a *precise* answer to the question how many QALYs a given span of life added up to. Faced with the sort of comparisons that the QALY approach requires, most people, I imagine, would say this sort of thing: 'Well, a year of normal life would certainly, for me, be worth at least eighteen months of life paralysed from the waist down, but it wouldn't be worth three years under those conditions.' In other words, most people would feel able to set numerical *limits* with some confidence—limits that would generally be narrower if they were judging for themselves than if they were judging for others. Now the point of the QALY approach is to help determine how resources should be allocated, especially as a matter of general policy. And for that purpose, it may be important to know *whether* renal dialysis, say, represents a better use of National Health Service funds than coronary bypass surgery; but it is probably not nearly so important, if important at all, to know just *how much* better. Suppose, then, one were to make the experiment of varying the numerical values one put into the equation, within the limits of what would strike one as intuitively reasonable. In many cases one would find that that made no difference to the *ordinal* conclusions that one ended up with, that is to say conclusions as to what was better than what. Such conclusions would then have the feature that economists sometimes describe as *robustness*—invariance with respect to adjustments of the input values, within the range of one's uncertainty. Thus, only a very radical scepticism, according to which one could not even, with any confidence, set numerical limits in such comparisons, would have the effect of rendering the QALY approach wholly useless. And such wholesale scepticism would, I should have thought, be very difficult convincingly to sustain.

III

Any sane moral theory is bound, it seems to me, to incorporate a welfarist element: other things being equal, it should be regarded as morally preferable to confer greater aggregate benefit than less. To this extent, it seems to me that QALY calculations, or something equivalent to them, should certainly be regarded as highly germane to the resolution of allocation problems within medicine. And, as I have just indicated, the fact that any assignment of precise QALY values is bound, in practice, to involve a degree of arbitrariness need not invalidate the qualitative conclusions that emerge, to the extent that the latter prove robust. But of course, it is one thing to say that welfarist considerations deserve to be given weight (great weight, even) in decisions regarding allocation, quite another to say that they should invariably be regarded as decisive.

The intuition from which we started was that medical resources should be allocated in such a way that they do the most good. But it is far from clear that 'the most good', here, should simply be equated with 'the greatest aggregate benefit'. And even if one thought it should, it is far from clear that allocation according to QALYs is what would best promote aggregate benefit, given that there are many things relevant to aggregate benefit that QALY calculations leave totally out of account.

If one reflects on what actually goes to determine the overall quality of one's life, one will find that this is dependent on many things that are likely to be overlooked in the rather crude quality of life indices used by the health care economists. This will include one's material and social circumstances: where one lives, what sort of job one has, if any, whether one lives alone or has a family—to what extent, in particular, one possesses those things that Rawls refers to as the 'social and material bases of self-respect'. But it will also include a host of less tangible things, some of them closely bound up with the latter. These will include, for example, one's temperament and psychological make-up in general, the character of one's relationships with others, the extent to which has a sense of security and of consonance between what one feels onself to be and what one finds oneself doing, and also a sense of being in command of one's life and of being free to pursue one's chosen projects, but neither effortlessly nor with too much fruitless struggle, and quite generally, the degree of stress, boredom and frustration, or satisfaction and fulfilment that is involved in day-to-day living.

There there is *social worth:* a calculation confined to QALYs leaves out of account the effects that deciding to treat this person rather than that might have on the lives of others—something that greatly exercises the doctors, Sir Patrick Cullen and Sir Colenso Ridgeon, in Shaw's play.

The situation is that Ridgeon has found a cure for tuberculosis, but only has the time, staff and laboratory facilities to take on one more patient. Two patients then present themselves. The one, Louis Dubedat, is an artist of genius but morally totally unscrupulous: he borrows money under false pretences which he never returns, and worse, turns out to be a bigamist. The other, Blenkinsop, is an impoversished doctor, hardworking and morally upright, but possessing no great skill or expertise. The following conversation ensues:

SIR PATRICK: Well, Mr. Saviour of Lives: which is it to be? that honest decent man Blenkinsop, or that rotten blackguard of an artist, eh?

RIDGEON: It's not an easy case to judge, is it? Blenkinsop's an honest decent man; but is he any use? Dubedat's a rotten blackguard; but he's a genuine source of pretty and pleasant and good things.

SIR PATRICK: What will he be a source of for that poor innocent wife of his, when she finds him out?

RIDGEON: That's true. Her life will be a hell.

SIR PATRICK: And tell me this. Suppose you had this choice put before you: either to go through life and find all the pictures bad but all the men and women good, or to go though life and find all the pictures good and all the men and women rotten. Which would you choose? . . . To me it's a plain choice between man and a lot of pictures.

RIDGEON: It's easier to replace a dead man than a good picture.[13]

Social worth will be highly sensitive to such considerations as whether one has dependants and, if so, how one's death would affect the quality of their lives, how important is the job one does, and how easy it would be to find someone else to do it comparably well.

There are economic considerations too. Some health care economists have advocated taking into account prospective earnings, on the grounds that if taxpayers' money is being used to pay for a given treatment its *real* cost (or real cost per QALY) will be less in the case of those patients treatment of whom will make the greatest positive impact on their net future contribution to government funds, and thus on the government's capacity to fund health care and welfare programmes generally. The economic cost, to the state, of someone's death or continued incapacitation also enters under this heading. I have seen it argued on this basis that, given a cardiac patient with dependants, incapacitated to the point of being unable to work, it may, all things being considered, actually be less costly for the state to pay for him to have a heart transplant (assuming this to be the only suitable treatment) than to allow him to die or continue living in a severely incapacitated state. (The point here is that if the transplant enables someone to return to work and support his family, then both he and they will cease to be a charge upon the state.) Such considerations may cast doubt on Alan Williams' conclusion, based on QALY calculations, that 'Heart transplantation does not seem to be a serious contender [for National Health Service funds]'.[14]

Save, perhaps, for the most intangible, all the broader types of welfarist consideration just surveyed have entered (in one centre or another) into decisions as to whom to select for some scarce life-saving procedure. So also have a number of other considerations having to do rather with some notion of *desert* (which will be sensitive to what one has done for society in the past, rather than what one is likely to do in the future). The Seattle 'God Committee' (officially, the Admissions and Policies Committee of the Seattle Artificial Kidney Center) is a case in point:

In selecting those to receive treatment, the Committee . . . considered . . . age, sex, marital status, and number of dependants, income, net worth, psychological stability, and past performance and future potential.[15]

[13] *The Doctor's Dilemma,* op. cit., 84–85.
[14] Alan Williams, op. cit., 328.
[15] Calebresi and Bobbit, op. cit., 233 n.

Michael Lockwood

Even from a welfarist perspective, however, it is far from clear that it is, all things considered, desirable that decisions about who should receive, e.g. renal dialysis, be made on this kind of basis. Consistent application of the broader sorts of criteria, especially the economic ones, is likely, in practice, to generate a heavy bias in favour of the white middle class, in a way that is potentially socially divisive.

(Actually, one finds just such a bias in the majority of British renal dialysis units. It is, for example, a fact in Britain, and a disturbing fact, that very few blacks receive renal dialysis, even though it is unlikely that racial discrimination, as such, has much to do with it—simply that the criteria employed tend *de facto* to exclude blacks. It seems unlikely, in fact, that this class/race/income bias has much to do even with doctors applying the kind of generalized quality of life considerations we have been surveying. What seems to be happening is that doctors prefer to give dialysis to those that their past experience suggests are most likely to do well on it. And statistically, educated middle class professionals are likely to do better than, say, unskilled labourers. They are, for example, likely to adhere more closely to the doctor's dietary and other instructions, and they tend to cope better with the psychological stress of being attached to a machine for a period of several hours two or three days a week.)

To the extent that such criteria are employed in a discretionary way at a microallocation level, a different kind of worry arises: is it really desirable that doctors should be allowed to sit in judgment on people's lives in the way that application of such a broad range of criteria implies? Do we want them to have that kind of power? Do we, in fact, want anyone to have that kind of power, even (or perhaps especially) the sort of predominantly lay panel set up in Seattle?[16] This sort of doubt may well be extended to QALY considerations too, if it is a matter of deciding, at a microallocation level, which of two rival contenders for some treatment is to get it. But the fact that QALYs are estimated mainly on the basis of quality of life as it is affected by a patient's overall health at any rate makes it something relatively objective, and something regarding which the doctor may at least claim some professional expertise—albeit that that expertise hardly extends to questions of the evaluative implications of these various health factors (the negative impact of which on the quality of people's lives there is evidence that doctors tend systematically to overestimate).[17]

[16] The Committee's membership 'consisted of a lawyer, a minister, a housewife, a banker, a state government official, a labor leader, and a surgeon' assisted by 'a medical advisory panel made up of personnel associated with the kidney treatment program' (Calebresi and Bobbit, op. cit., 209 n.).
[17] Alan Williams, op. cit., 327.

44

IV

But I mention all these other sorts of welfarist consideration mainly to put them to one side. For what I really want to focus on here is the philosophically more fundamental objection that can be levelled against the QALY approach: namely that, precisely *because* it is uncompromisingly welfarist, it is in principle liable to result in forms of allocation that are *unjust* or *unfair*.

I shall not attempt here to define justice or unfairness. (All of the well-known philosophical theories of justice seem to me to be subject to decisive objections; and yet I have no alternative theory to offer.) Intuitively, however, justice has something to do with equality, and something also to do with giving appropriate weight to certain sorts of moral *claim*. From a commonsense point of view, the fact that A could confer some benefit, X, on B does not, as such, give B any claim upon A. Only if it is a particular kind of benefit, and A has a particular kind of responsibility for B, does it follow that A is even *prima facie* morally obliged to confer X upon B, or, consequently, that his refusal to do so constitutes any kind of injustice towards B. Now, continuing in this rather abstract vein, the claim that any patient would plausibly be thought to have on the health services (or on the state, in so far as it in turn is responsible for the health of its citizens) is a function not so much of the amount of *benefit* that the health services are in a position to confer, as of the person's health *needs* in relation to the services' capacity effectively to meet those needs.

One reason, then, why the QALY approach can strike one as intuitively unjust is that the principle 'To each according to what will generate the most QALYs' is potentially in conflict with the principle 'To each according to his need'. A patient suffering from end-stage renal failure may be said to *need* dialysis or a kidney transplant, just as a patient with an arthritic hip *needs* a hip replacement. But the first patient's need is clearly the greater. Following David Wiggins,[18] one can think of the degree to which a person, P, needs something, X, as a function of the degree to which his lack of X compromises P's capacity to flourish as a human being ('flourishing' now being, in British philosophical circles, the most favoured translation of Aristotle's *eudaimonia*). Someone, then, who will die without some particular treatment needs it in the strongest possible sense; for one cannot flourish at all if one is dead. Other things being equal, one would think, the greater the need the weightier the claim on available resources. But the QALY arithmetic is inherently insensitive to differences in degree

[18] David Wiggins, 'Claims of Need', in Ted Honderich (ed.), *Morality and Objectivity* (London: Routledge & Kegan Paul, 1984), 149–202.

of need, except in so far as they happen to correlate with the degree of benefit per unit cost that treatment can confer. It attaches just as much value to the QALYs generated by treating those in a state of lesser need as it does to those generated by treating those in a state of greater need.

Indeed, it is arguable that some forms of medical treatment, whilst they confer a genuine benefit, do not minister to any *need,* as such, at all. I have in mind, for example, cosmetic surgery designed to remove normal wrinkles from the faces of middle-aged ladies. A model or an actress might, to be sure, need such an operation if she was to flourish, if the wrinkles compromised her ability to find employment (and so might a woman who was neurotically obsessed with her looks, if the operation could remove the obsession). But for the rest, the wrinkles do not compromise their capacity to flourish; it is merely that, with the operation, they may be enabled to flourish at a higher level. Such operations are, in short, a luxury. Suppose, then, as seems to me entirely possible, that some health care economist were able to show that facelifts, say, generated even more QALYs per unit cost than do hip-replacement operations. Would anyone really think that was sufficient reason for switching resources from hip replacements towards such cosmetic surgery?

Surely not. And if not, then by the same token it is far from clear that the QALY calculations cited by Williams constitute a sufficient reason for transferring resources from renal dialysis to hip replacements. One could plausibly argue that someone who will die, if he or she doesn't receive a certain form of treatment, has an intrinsically much stronger claim on available resources than someone whose life is not at stake, even if there is a sense in which greater aggregate benefit could be achieved by neglecting those whose life was threatened in favour of those suffering from reduced mobility or discomfort. And if so, then the greater moral weight that attaches to the claim could be held to outweigh the greater cost of the life-saving treatment per unit QALY generated.

Another respect in which allocation according to QALYs can result in modes of allocation which would intuitively seem unjust is that it will tend, in certain circumstances, to favour those who are (from a health point of view) already relatively fortunate over those who are less fortunate. This, indeed, was the force of the example cited earlier, where it was pointed out that the logic of QALYs would work to the disadvantage of elderly arthritic patients. But I want, for the moment, to set aside the age factor, since it raises important points of principle in its own right which are better dealt with separately. Let us simply suppose that there are two candidates for renal dialysis, and that the only relevant difference between them is that one is suffering from arthritis and the other is not. Assume that the quality of life of the arthritic patient is significantly impaired by his arthritis, but that there is no reason to suppose that it will in any way affect the chances of the dialysis proving successful. Assume, further, that both patients have an equally intense wish to go on living. Under these circumstances, the QALY approach says: give the dialysis to the patient who does not have arthritis. For every extra year of life we give him will correspond to a higher QALY value than a year given to the other.

There is a clear sense in which this is inequitable, for what it amounts to is taking the fact that someone is already unfortunate, in one respect, as a reason for visiting further misfortunes upon him (or at least denying him benefits). One might reasonably ask whether it was consistent with natural justice to allocate life-saving resources on the basis: 'From him who hath not shall be taken away even that which he hath', namely his life.

In such cases as this, I find myself in agreement with John Harris's assertion that allocation by QALYs 'amounts to unjust discrimination between individuals'. On the other hand, if doctors are faced with a choice of treating either of two patients, who are in an equivalent state of need, it does not seem to me unjust to choose to treat the patient for whom the treatment is more likely to prove successful. Nor does it seem to me unjust to prefer to treat the patient who can be treated at less cost, whether at the level of microallocation or macroallocation. Harris, by contrast, finds this an objectionable feature of the QALY approach:

> If a 'high priority health care activity is one where the cost-per-QALY is low and a low priority is one where cost-per-QALY is high' then people who just happen to have conditions which are relatively cheap to treat are always to be given priority over those who happen to have conditions which are relatively expensive to treat. This will inevitably involve not only a systematic pattern of disadvantage to particular groups of patients, or to people afflicted with particular diseases or conditions, but perhaps also a systematic preference for the survival of some kinds of patients at the expense of others. We usually think that justice requires that we do not allow certain sections of the community or certain types of individual to become the victims of systematic disadvantage . . .[19]

This line of reasoning seems to me fallacious. The principal basis of just dealing in a health care context is, surely, that people are thought of as having a claim on available health care resources that is proportional to their degree of need. (In the absence, that is, of other considerations

[19] John Harris, 'Rationing Life: Quality or Justice' (unpublished), paper presented to the British Medical Association Annual Scientific Meeting, Oxford, 10–12 April 1986, p. 9.

bearing upon what is just or fair.) From this point of view, if two patients (whether suffering from the same or different diseases) are equally in need of treatment, then they have the same claim on available resources. In the context of finite resources, this implies that if the resources required to treat them effectively are the same, neither has a better claim to being treated than the other (again, in the absence of other considerations). But if the resources required to treat the one are greater than those required to treat the other, it is perfectly compatible with recognizing that they have an equal claim on resources to say that the patient whose treatment requires a lesser expenditure of resources should be treated to the exclusion of the other.

Putting it schematically, suppose that the two patients, Andrew and Brian, in virtue of their health needs, were both thought to have a claim on medical resources of weight W, and that effective treatment of Andrew would call for an expenditure of resources X, whereas effective treatment of Brian would call for an expenditure of resources Y, where Y is less than X. (Any claim on resources is, after all, clearly going to be contingent on their effectiveness in ministering to the need that grounds the claim.) It is then entirely consistent with recognizing that they both have a prior claim of weight W to say that Brian should be treated in preference to Andrew. For what that implies is that, in the circumstances, a claim of weight W carries with it an entitlement to an expenditure of resources Y (conditional upon its being effective), but not to the larger expenditure of resources X. And that is surely perfectly reasonable. Indeed, to devote a disproportionate amount of one's health care resources to the treatment of people in a given state of need, when a lesser expenditure would enable one effectively to treat more people in an equivalent or greater state of need, would itself, from this point of view, be a violation of the principle that the claim on resources is proportional to need.

I do not, incidentally, think it is true, *absolutely in general,* that 'justice requires that we do not allow certain sections of the community to become the victims of systematic disadvantage'. If it were true, then justice would require, absurdly, that we not allow, say, more able people to get better jobs. What justice actually requires is that we do not discriminate between people on the basis of unjust criteria—race and sex being obvious cases in point. Thus if someone claims, as Harris does, that it is unjust to allocate health care on the basis of how great an expenditure of resources is required to minister effectively to a given need, the burden is on him to show that this *particular* criterion is unjust. But this he does not attempt to do; and the argument I have just presented seems to lead to quite the opposite conclusion, that it is perfectly just. This is not to deny, of course, that it is thoroughly bad luck if someone finds himself suffering from a condition the treatment for which is just too expensive to constitute a justifiable use of limited health care resources. But bad luck is not, *ipso facto,* injustice.

I alluded, in passing, to 'other considerations' that might be thought relevant to justice. Given two people who are equally in need of a given form of treatment, some would think it morally appropriate to take into account the fact that one of them has, through irresponsible behaviour, brought his condition upon himself. An example which featured in a recent television programme on the allocation of renal dialysis[20] was that of a patient suffering from renal failure consequent upon drug abuse (though it should have been pointed out, on this programme, that a history of drug abuse may, for purely medical reasons, cause difficulties when it comes to dialysis). For my own part, I am somewhat sceptical about the claim that *justice* requires that one should be sensitive to this kind of consideration. And this is because I am sceptical about free will. I am personally inclined to think that, in an important sense, we are all of us victims of our genetic inheritance, upbringing and so forth, and that it is not true that people who bring certain kinds of health care need on themselves—e.g. by driving dangerously, over-eating, smoking or abusing drugs or alcohol—really *could,* in the final analysis, have acted any differently. (That said, I have heard it argued that there might be good welfarist reasons for according the claims of such people on health care resources a relatively low priority, if the fact were to be widely publicized and could act as an effective deterrent to such irresponsible behaviour. But I doubt whether it would. Someone who is undeterred by the prospect of seriously damaging his health is hardly likely, in my opinion, to be deterred by the prospect of less than ideal health care thereafter. An alternative and more promising pro-posal might be to give people some kind of tax incentive towards healthy living—say, in a British context, by making National Insurance payments depend in some degree on doctor's reports, so that someone who was overweight or who smoked, for example, would find himself paying more. But such a scheme might prove, in practice, very difficult to administer satisfactorily.)

A second point on which I find myself in disagreement with Harris concerns the relevance of *age* to allocation questions. Harris[21] maintains that it is *ageist* to take the fact that one of two rival contenders for renal dialysis, say, is younger as a reason for preferring to treat him, ageism, here, meaning wilful discrimination on the basis of age, parallel to

---

[20] In the *Doctor's Dilemma* series, Granada Television, 1984.
[21] Harris, op. cit., 8. This line of thought is developed at greater length in his *The Value of Life: An Introduction to Medical Ethics* (London: Routledge & Kegan Paul, 1985), Ch. 5.

racism, sexism and, most recently, speciesism (taking the fact that an animal does not belong to the human species as a reason for saying that its suffering, say, matters less than equivalent suffering in the case of a human being). Now it goes without saying that some ways of taking someone's age into account, whether in a health care context or elsewhere, would be unjust. But I do not think it is unjust to allocate life-extending treatment on the basis that the younger one is, the weightier, other things being equal, is one's claim upon available resources.

The reason I say this is that I am impressed, as Harris is not, by what is commonly referred to as the 'fair innings argument'. The thought here, which seems to me absolutely correct, is that an older person seeking dialysis, for example, has already by definition lived for longer than a younger person. To treat the older person, letting the younger person die, would thus be inherently inequitable in terms of years of life lived: the younger person would get no more years than the relatively few he has already had, whereas the older person, who has already had more than the younger person, will get several years more.

Of course, this argument only works if one takes seriously the identity of persons over time. If one does not, then one can mount a counter-argument parallel to that which led us to the conclusion that it is inequitable to take the fact that someone has arthritis, for example, as a contraindication, in a situation of scarcity, to providing him with life-extending treatment. 'It is bad enough being old', someone might argue. 'To cite that as a reason for denying life-saving measures is to take the fact that one is already unfortunate in one respect as a reason for imposing yet a further misfortune, namely death. How can that be fair?' Well, quite easily; it is fair, inasmuch as the person referred to has already had a reasonably long life, longer, anyway, than that of rival contenders for the treatment. Fairness must be assessed on the basis of someone's life as a whole, unless one thinks of each 'time-slice' of a person as an independent contender for available resources, which would seem to me perverse. (But then I am not a sceptic about personal identity. Someone who took a more sceptical position than I, such as that defended by Derek Parfit in his influential *Reasons and Persons*,[22] might well be disposed to find great merit in the counter-argument to the fair innings argument that I have just cited.)

I mentioned earlier the fact that, from a welfarist perspective, it would be appropriate to take into consideration whether a patient had dependants, and if so how many and of what age—something that is not taken into account in a QALY calculation. How does this criterion look

[22] Derek Parfit, *Reasons and Persons* (Oxford University Press, 1984), Part III.

from the standpoint of justice? Well it depends, it seems to me, on the precise grounds on which the interests of dependants are included in the equation. The central principle of justice that is operative here, I have been suggesting, is that one's claim on resources is proportional to one's need (in the absence of other factors). Now such a principle not only permits but actually requires one to take dependants into account, to the extent that these dependants themselves have a stake in the life or health of the patient *that itself amounts to a need,* in the strong sense of that term. What one must ask, then, is whether the death or continued ill-health of the patient compromises the capacity of these dependants to flourish as human beings. If it does, then the health care needs of the patient are, in an extended sense, their health care needs too, and should be taken into account as such. Under such circumstances one may favour a mother with young children over a single person in an equivalent state of need, not because she herself has a greater claim on health care resources than does the single person, but because her children have, in virtue of their own need of the mother, claims in their own right—claims which can only be satisfied (or at least which can best be satisfied) through treating her.

Both here and as regards whether one should take age into account, it therefore seems to me that welfarist considerations, on the one hand, and considerations having to do with justice, on the other, will tend to converge on the same conclusion. (QALY calculations, as we have seen, tend statistically to favour the young for life-extending treatment, on grounds of life expectancy, quality of life, as gauged in terms of distress and disability, and also, in the case of renal dialysis, on the basis of the prospects for an eventual transplant.) Here the conclusions may be 'robust' in a new, wider sense: they may be invariant with respect to variations in one's moral assumptions, whether uncompromisingly welfarist or highly sensitive to considerations of justice.

But I see no particular reason to suppose that in general one will find any such convergence between justice and welfare (though there are many philosophers who argue that our intuitions about what is just are likely in practice to converge with what welfarism would enjoin, when we take sufficiently many factors into account in our welfarist calculations, or, like Richard Hare, that our intuitions about what is just are intuitions that it is, by and large, best from a welfarist point of view for people to have and act upon).[23] What then, since I have argued that any sane moral theory must include a welfarist element, should happen

[23] Hare's theory was originally put forward in R. M. Hare, 'Ethical Theory and Utilitarianism', in H. D. Lewis (ed.), *Contemporary Moral Philosophy 4* (London: Allen and Unwin, 1976); it is developed in greater detail in his *Moral Thinking* (Oxford University Press, 1981).

when justice and welfare come into conflict with each other, as I have argued that they do, in many QALY calculations? To give a wholly general answer to this question is as difficult as giving a theory of justice in the first place. But, at the level of moral phenomenology, it would seem that, over a considerable middle range of cases, where the cost in welfarist terms of giving priority to considerations of justice is not that enormous, we think it morally appropriate to favour justice. Indeed, one could view justice as *constraining* one's pursuit of welfarist aims: it is morally legitimate, indeed laudable, to aim for greater aggregate benefit, *provided* one acts justly in the pursuit of that aim.

One logical mechanism whereby justice can thus constrain welfarism may be via Joseph Raz's interesting concept of *exclusionary reasons*. An exclusionary reason is a reason for *not* taking something else as a reason. For example, justice gives the judge in a court of law a reason for not taking as a reason for giving a lenient sentence the fact that the accused is an old friend. Indeed, the image of justice as standing blindfold is a perfect symbolic embodiment of this notion of exclusionary reasons. Now in the context of the allocation of scarce lifesaving therapy, our earlier arguments might suggest that justice should be blind, for example, to the patient's quality of life, in respects that have nothing to do with the likely effectiveness of the treatment or the patient's wish to go on living.

This notion of justice as constraining welfarism constitutes the element of truth in John Rawls' claim that justice should be given what he calls *lexical priority* over other values, such as efficiency,[24] by which he means that the demands of justice have to be met before one starts discriminating amongst different policies or courses of action on other grounds: any policy or course of action which violates justice is excluded at the outset. But that, whilst it may be the right way to look at matters in a middle range of cases, becomes grossly implausible if insisted upon right across the board. It is moral fanaticism to say, with William Watson, 'Fiat justitia et ruant coeli' (Let justice be done though the heavens fall) or with the Emperor Ferdinand I, 'Fiat justitia, et pereat mundi' (Let justice be done, though the world perish). Whilst differences in quality of life should perhaps, in the name of justice, be ignored over a large middle range of cases, when allocating scarce resources, there comes a point where differences in prospective distress and disability are so great that it would be morally irresponsible not to take them into account, on welfarist grounds. And of course one ought, by the logic of what I have been saying, to take such factors into account when choosing amongst policies or courses of action which are none of them unjust. What I have been proposing is a pluralistic scheme of

---

[24] John Rawls, *A Theory of Justice* (Oxford University Press, 1973), para. 8.

values in which welfare is one amongst a number of elements, which will also include justice, autonomy, and no doubt other things too. We should not let enthusiasm for QALYs blind us to these other values, nor let the fact that unconstrained maximization of QALYs may be a recipe for injustice blind us to the crucial importance of the welfarist considerations that QALY calculations embody. The allocation of scarce medical resources is an area where rationality is sorely called for, where we urgently need to examine our priorities in the light of argument and evidence of their relative efficacy. As a contribution to this task—but only as a contribution, not the last word on allocation matters—QALYs are greatly to be welcomed.

Postscript 1987[25]

Since writing this article, I have come to think (partly as a result of some very stimulating conversations with John Broome) that what I say in response to John Harris's claims needs to be amended. Harris, as we have seen, argues that a policy of thoroughgoing QALY maximization is ageist, and to that extent unjust. My response in the text was to argue that this is not unjust, and that, from the standpoint of justice, we ought, other things being equal, to favour younger patients in the allocation of scarce life-saving resources. What I should now argue is that Harris is mistaken in thinking that the QALY approach is ageist. For it is not true that QALY maximization involves discriminating against older patients as such; what it discriminates against are those with relatively low life expectancy, given that that they receive the treatment. The situation is parallel to that of selecting amongst applicants for a job that calls for a high degree of physical strength. In such circumstances, men would be most likely to be chosen in preference to women; but that would not be sexist, provided that weaker men were not chosen in preference to demonstratively stronger women. Clearly, the QALY approach is not committed to selecting younger people in preference to older people that demonstrably have a higher post-treatment life expectancy. But that very fact now seems to me to be an objection to unconstrained QALY maximization. For if, as I have been arguing, the fair innings argument is sound, then one ought, in the name of fairness, to prefer a younger over an older patient, for life-saving treatment, even if the post-treatment life-expectancy of the younger patient is no greater than that of the older patient. As I now see

[25] The preceding text appears originally in French in the *Revue de Méta-physique et de Morale*, No. 3/1987, 307–328. The postscript which follows has been added for this volume.

Michael Lockwood

it, what is objectionable, here, about unconstrained QALY maximization, is not that it involves discriminating on the basis of age, but, on the contrary, that it fails to take age into account in circumstances where, in fairness, it ought to do so. It fails to be ageist when it should be, rather than being ageist when it should not.

The second point involves Harris's claim that it is unfair, when faced with limited resources, to favour patients that can be treated at less cost. In the article I argued that this was not unfair to the patients who needed relatively costly treatment; but merely a case of bad luck. Now, however, I am inclined to think that this is, after all, unfair, but that to treat a smaller number of people at greater cost, at the expense of failing to treat a larger number of equally needy patients, would be more unfair still. Suppose Tom, Dick and Harriet are in a state of equal need, and that for each of their conditions there exists a unique corresponding treatment that will be wholly effective. However, Tom's treatment costs £6,000, whereas Dick's and Harriet's both cost £3,000. Suppose, further, that nothing useful can be done for these patients for any amounts less than these, and that there is only £6,000 in the kitty. Given that they are all equally needy, Tom, Dick and Harriet each have, *a priori,* an equal claim on available resources. But we cannot just split the money three ways, since £2,000 will not, for any of them, buy effective treatment. By treating Dick and Harriet, at the expense of Tom, we are, it seems to me, being unfair to Tom, since his need is the same as that of Dick and Harriet, and yet he gets nothing. But in treating Tom, at the expense of Dick and Harriet, we would be being even more unfair, since then two of them would get nothing; and the numerical disparity between the actual allocation of resources and the unattainable ideal of £2,000 worth of effective treatment apiece, would be twice as great, in this case. The fairest thing we could do, in this situation, would be to have a weighted lottery, in which Tom was given a one-third chance of getting treated, at a cost of £6,000, while Dick and Harriet were given a two-thirds chance of being treated, at £3,000 apiece. For then the *expected* resource allocation, that is say the probability of getting treated multiplied by the cost, would be the same for all of them, namely £2,000, thus matching their equal need. But even that is not perfectly fair, since it ameliorates but does not eliminate the inevitable inequality of the final outcome.

Two final points. First, I quite deliberately say 'unfair' here, rather than 'unjust'. We are sometimes it seems to me, faced with situations in which whatever we do will result in an outcome that is, to some extent, unfair. But it strikes me as a bit odd to describe it as unjust. We might perhaps say that an outcome is perfectly just when it reduces unfairness to the absolute minimum that the situation allows. But anyway, a pattern of distribution of scarce médical resources that, other things being equal, will favour those who can be treated at less cost, is not perfectly just if, as I now believe, a weighted lorry would be fairer. Nevertheless, I should not advocate such a lottery. First, it would be an administrative nightmare. But secondly, it would be significantly less efficient at generating QALYs. Given that, in any case, considerations of justice have, to some extent, to be weighed against welfarist considerations, I would judge that favouring those who can be treated at less cost gives about the right weight to both.

Good, Fairness and QALYs

JOHN BROOME

I

Counting QALYs (quality adjusted life years) has been proposed as a way of deciding how resources should be distributed in the health service: put resources where they will produce the most QALYs. This proposal has encountered strong opposition. There has been a disagreement between some economists[1] favouring QALYs and some philosophers[2] opposing them. But the argument has, I think, mostly been at cross-purposes. Those in favour of QALYs point out what they can do, and those against point out what they can't. There need be no disagreement about this. What is needed is to sort out what is the proper domain of QALYs, and it may be possible to do this amicably. Then we may be able to get on with the more useful job of deciding how well QALYs perform within their domain. In this paper I shall try to accomplish the first task (sections II–IV), and make a start on the second (sections V–VIII).

QALYs are aimed at assessing the *total of good*. The main objection to them—at least this is John Harris's[3] main objection—is that they do not properly take account of *justice or fairness in the distribution of good*. But that is not what they are aimed at. Assessing the total of good is worthwhile, and it has a part to play in allocating resources. Only it is not everything.

What I have just said is inaccurate. Fairness is itself a good and unfairness a harm. If good is distributed unfairly that in itself reduces the total of good. More accurately, I should say that QALYs are aimed at assessing the total of good excluding fairness. From now on, though, when I speak of good I am to be understood as referring to good excluding fairness. QALYs are aimed at good in this sense.

In distributing resources, the total of good done is one consideration and fairness is another. Both count. It is true that in some moral

---

[1] For instance, Alan Williams 'The Value of QALYS', *Health and Social Services Journal* 18 July 1985.

[2] For instance, John Harris, 'Rationing Life: Quality or Justice', notes presented for a lecture to the British Medical Association Annual Scientific Meeting, 1986. Cf. John Harris, *The Value of Life* (London: Routledge & Kegan Paul, 1985), 89.

[3] Ibid.

theories fairness is not treated as a separate consideration. This seems to be true of utilitarianism, for instance. One view of utilitarianism is that it attaches no value to fairness. Another is that utilitarianism is itself an account of fairness, so that to maximize good is itself to be fair according to utilitarianism.[4] Either way, once good is maximized there is no need to be concerned about the fairness of its distribution. This has often been seen as a difficulty with utilitarianism; it seems to offend intuition.

It may be that some of the friends of QALYs take a utilitarian line. They may not acknowledge that there is a goal, fairness, that QALYs cannot take account of. If so, the right response is to point out that there is this separate goal, and that QALYs cannot determine completely what the distribution of resources should be. They may be important none the less. The wrong response is to deny the value of QALYs even in assessing good, or to suggest that QALYs are pernicious because they do not take account of fairness. What is unattractive about utilitarianism is that it does not separate the two goals of good and fairness. In responding to it, therefore, it is important not to muddle up these goals yourself. It would be helpful, too, to produce an account of fairness that explains properly what fairness requires in the distribution of resources, and how it can be a separate goal. In a moment I shall outline an account of this sort.

John Harris does not properly separate the consideration of fairness from the consideration of total good. This leads him to make several false statements. He says:[5]

> [1] All people who wish to go on living, however uncomfortable their continued existence may be, however many friends and relations they have, however long or short that existence may be expected to be, have each of them something that is of equal value to them-selves—call it the rest of their lives. [2] Each is equally wronged if their lives are cut needlessly short, that is, if their lives are not prolonged when they want them to be and when they could be. Whatever the rest of our lives might be expected to be like, so long as we want our lives to continue, then [3] we each suffer the same misfortune, and [4] are wronged in the same way when that wish is deliberately frustrated by others.

Statement [4] is true in one sense; we are all wronged in the same way if we are prevented from living, namely the way of being prevented from living. Statements [1], [2] and [3] are all false.

Take [1] first. The notion of the value to a person of some object is a fairly flexible one. One possible sense is how much the person wants it.

---

[4] James Griffin, 'Some Problems of Fairness', *Ethics* **96** (1985), 100–118.
[5] Op.cit.

But amongst people who want their lives to continue, some want that more than others. Another possible sense is how valuable the person believes the object to be. But amongst people who want their lives to continue, some think their lives more valuable than others think theirs. So in neither of these senses is the value to a person of the rest of her life the same for everybody. There may be other senses, but I am sure there are none that would make proposition [1] true.

Next [2]. It is debatable what wrong or wrongs are done a person in cutting her life needlessly short. Amongst the wrongs done her may be an injustice and, possibly, this may be an equal wrong for everybody. But also amongst the wrongs is the wrong of depriving her of good. The good she is deprived of is the difference between how good her life would have been had she continued to live and how good it is, being cut needlessly short. This difference is not the same for everybody. So not everybody is equally wronged by having their lives needlessly cut short.

Finally [3]. Some people suffer a greater loss of good than others if their wish to live is frustrated; I have just said that. So they suffer a greater misfortune.

What leads Harris to advance these falsehoods? What he wishes to say, I think, is that everybody suffers the same injustice or the same unfairness if their lives are cut short. This may or may not be right, but it is a lot more plausible than what he does say. It might be filled out (in the manner of my account of fairness below) by saying that everyone has an equal claim to life, so they suffer an equal unfairness if their claim is overridden. This need not make any reference to good. But Harris speaks instead of value, wrong and misfortune, all things that, at least partly, have to do with good. He seems to be himself in the grip of the utilitarian view that what is fair must be determined by what is good.

II

Now my account of fairness. This will only be an outline, because I have presented a fuller account in another article.[6] The principal evidence I have to offer in support of the account is that it is, I believe, the only way to explain adequately the value of random selection. When an indivisible good such as haemodialysis is to be distributed and there is not enough to go round everybody who needs it, it sometimes seems

[6] John Broome, 'Fairness and the Random Distribution of Goods', in Jon Elster (ed.), *Justice and the Lottery* (Cambridge University Press, forthcoming). See also John Broome, 'Selecting People Randomly, *Ethics* **95** (1984), 56–67.

best to distribute it randomly. This may be so even when there is a balance of reasons in favour of some candidates rather than others. Some candidates, for instance, may be younger, and therefore stand to gain more from haemodialysis. It will give them more years of life than it gives older candidates. Even so, a lottery may be the best way to choose. My account explains why this is so, and I can find no other account that does so adequately. I shall describe it now without much argument. But I hope it has some plausibility on its own.

Suppose a good, divisible or not, is to be distributed amongst some candidates. It might be haemodialysis, or it might be the general resources of the health service, or any other good. For each candidate there will be reasons why she should have the good, or some of it. For instance, there will be utilitarian reasons. The utilitarian reason in favour of a particular candidate's getting it is the good that would be done by her getting it. This would include the extra good she would enjoy in her own life as a result, and the extra good that would come to other people such as her family. And there may be other reasons too. Some of the candidates, for instance, may be *entitled* to some of the good, perhaps because they have earned it.

How should the good be distributed? One view is that it should go to the candidates for whom there are the strongest reasons that they should get it. For a divisible good, this criterion should be applied one small unit at a time. To explain this, and to make the explanation simple, I shall suppose we are dealing with utilitarian reasons only, but the idea is general. The first unit of health resources (if that is what is in question) should go to the person whose getting it would do the most good; the second unit to the person whose getting that would do the most good, and so on. Call the good done by allocating a small unit of resources to a person, on top of what she already has, her 'marginal benefit'. The process I am describing gives each extra unit of resources to the person with the greatest marginal benefit. It often seems plausible that a person's marginal benefit will diminish as the resources she receives increase. If so, the process will spread the resources amongst the candidates, and end up by equalizing all their marginal benefits. This will ensure that the maximum possible good is done by the resources available. More generally, if there are other reasons in question besides good, it will maximize the satisfaction of reasons.

If the good is indivisible, according to this view, each unit should still go to the person for whom the reasons are strongest that she should have it. This would again maximize the satisfaction of reasons. In practice, with a good like haemodialysis, the weighing of reasons is very difficult, and if it is done deliberately by a person or a committee there are dangers of prejudice and corruption. The right thing in this case is to find a way of maximizing the satisfaction of reasons as well as possible on average. For instance, making it a rule to give haemodialysis to the youngest candidates would do quite well. By and large there will be better reasons for treating younger candidates than older because, as I have said, the younger stand to gain more.

I shall call the view that this is the right thing to do the 'weighing' or 'maximizing' view. Utilitarianism is a special case of it, the case that only acknowledges good as a reason. On the whole, when it comes to distributing health resources, one would expect utilitarianism to concentrate them on the young, where they will do the most good. It would concentrate them entirely on the young were it not for diminishing marginal benefit. The old will only get a look in when the young have been so well served that the marginal benefit of treating them has diminished to the level of the marginal benefit of starting to treat the old.

This seems unfair. The trouble with the maximizing view is that it pays no attention to fairness.

III

To understand fairness, we must start by dividing the reasons why a person should have a good into two classes: claims and other reasons. By a claim I mean a duty owed to the person herself that she should have the good. There can certainly be reasons that are not claims. Suppose, for instance, that a person has offered to endow a new hospital if only she is given haemodialysis. This is a reason for giving her haemodialysis, but it is not a claim on her part. Her offer does not mean it is owed to her to give her the treatment.

It is not easy to produce a general theory of which reasons are claims and which are not. And it is a controversial matter. I shall not attempt it. I shall only talk about the right response to claims, not about where claims come from.

Claims are the object of fairness. Fairness is concerned with mediating between the claims of different people. It is not concerned with reasons that are not claims. If there is a reason why someone should get a good, but she does not get it, she is not treated unfairly unless the reason was a claim. She is not treated unfairly if no duty was owed her in the first place that she should have it.

In mediating between claims, then, what does fairness require? It is not enough simply to give claims their proper weight in comparing them with other reasons and the claims of other people. That is no more than the maximizing view. Nor is it enough to give claims extra weight compared with other reasons. Suppose, for the sake of argument, that everyone has an equal claim to medical resources. Then, when allocat-

John Broome

ing resources by weighing reasons, everyone's claims will cancel out, however much weight is given them. The decision will depend only on other reasons. The result will coincide with the maximizing view again. Medical resources will mostly go to the young. But now, given the assumption that everyone's claims are equal, this really does seem decidedly unfair. The equal claims, which is all that fairness is concerned with, have made no difference at all.

When several people have claims to a good, these conflicting claims are duties owed to different people. Sometimes there can be a conflict of duties owed to a single person: the duty to be truthful may conflict with the duty to spare her distress, for instance. These duties we weigh against each other in deciding what to do. To weigh conflicting claims against each other, and against other reasons, is to treat them in the same way as we treat duties owed to the same person. It does not, I think, give enough attention to the fact that they are duties owed to different people. Fairness is about mediating between different people: no issue of fairness arises over mediating conflicting duties when they are owed to a single person. That, I think, is why fairness requires more than weighing.

What does it require, then? I think it requires that *claims should actually be satisfied in proportion to their strength.* There are two essential points to this formula. First, it is actual satisfaction that is needed, not mere consideration or weighing. Second, what fairness requires is a relative matter. It is not concerned with the total of satisfaction, but with how well one person's claim is satisfied compared with other people's. For one thing, equal claims should be equally satisfied. If several people have equal claims to a good, they are treated perfectly fairly if, and only if, they all get equal amounts. This is true even if they all get very little or even none at all. (The more they get the better, of course, but not the fairer.) Also, stronger claims should be satisfied more than less strong ones, but less strong claims should be satisfied to some extent. It is unfair simply to override weaker claims in favour of stronger ones, and not satisfy them at all.

Suppose, once again for the sake of argument, that all the candidates for haemodialysis have the same claim, but they cannot all receive the treatment. Then fairness can only be perfectly satisfied by treating none of them. This would presumably be so wasteful that it is not the best solution. But then, if some people are treated and others are not, some unfairness is inevitable. I argued in my other paper[7] that the unfairness can be mitigated by holding a lottery, which gives everyone an equal chance. Getting a chance, although it does not really satisfy

[7] Op.cit.

one's claim to treatment, is a sort of surrogate satisfaction that is better than no satisfaction at all.

The idea that equal claims demand equal satisfaction, or more generally that claims demand proportional satisfaction, is very natural. But it is very radically in conflict with the maximizing view. It denies that there is anything that should be maximized. It even denies that fairness should be maximized. Suppose, for the sake of argument once more, that everyone has an equal claim to medical resources. It would be fairest, then, for these resources to be equally distributed. But suppose they are not; suppose the young have the lion's share. And suppose a small amount of extra resources become available. The greatest fairness would be achieved by devoting all these resources to the old; this will bring the overall distribution as near as possible to equality. But the young have some claim to these extra resources. Their claim is not as strong as the claim of the old, because they already have more resources devoted to them, but it is implausible that they have no claim at all.[8] Therefore, according to the proportional satisfaction formula, fairness requires that they should get some.

The proportional satisfaction formula is non-maximizing or, to put it another way, non-consequentialist. In one sense, it says it is generally wrong to do what there is the best reason to do (though of course, in another sense, it does itself provide a reason for doing what it says is right).

IV

Now what, actually, does this account say about the distribution of medical resources? This depends on what claims people actually have

[8] The only way of avoiding the non-consequentialist conclusion I am describing would be to suppose, in this example, that the young have no claim at all to the extra resources, because they already have more than their fair share. On some occasions a view like this might be right. But it cannot in general reconcile my proportional satisfaction formula with maximizing fairness. If everyone has an equal claim to a good, and their shares are actually unequal, and a small extra quantity of the good becomes available, fairness would be maximized by giving it to the person who has least. The proportional satisfaction formula, on the other hand, would say this was the fairest thing to do only if no one else has any claim at all. But it is incredible that no one else should have a claim. Suppose that, actually, the extra quantity goes to the person who already has the most. This would be unfair to the person who has the least. But if no one apart from this person has any claim at all, then it is unfair to no one else. But it is surely also unfair at least to the person who is second from the bottom.

on medical resources. I shall not take sides on this but mention some possible views. One is that everybody has an equal claim. Fairness would then require the resources to be equally distributed. Another is that claims on medical resources are determined by need.[9] This means that, by and large, older people will have stronger claims than younger because they need the resources more. So fairness requires them to get a larger share.

Yet another view is that a person's claim depends on the amount of good she can derive from the resources. By and large, this will give younger people a stronger claim than older. This is a sort of utilitarian view. Utilitarians disagree about claims. All utilitarians believe we have a duty to maximize good, but only some believe this is a duty owed to the people whose good it is.[10] If it is a duty owed to these people, then it is a claim. However, no utilitarian will draw the conclusion that follows according to my account: that fairness requires resources to be distributed in proportion to the good they will do. Utilitarianism says that good should be maximized, which is something else entirely. It says that claims should simply be weighed against each other in the maximizing calculation. Weaker claims will be overriden by stronger ones. But according to my account, fairness prohibits that and will do so even if one takes a utilitarian view about the strength of people's claims. People who can derive less good from medical resources, perhaps because they are old and will not live long anyway, will have weaker claims according to this view. But even they should get their share.

Fairness, though, is not everything. In deciding how to distribute a good, fairness is opposed to acting simply on the basis of the strongest reasons. But the reason why a person should have a good are, nevertheless, *reasons*. Responding to them must be a consideration in distributing resources. This is the maximizing consideration. Fairness and maximizing will normally pull in different directions, and they need to be balanced against each other. Neither is overriding. It will almost certainly be right to sacrifice some good in total for the sake of fairness. And it will almost certainly be right to tolerate some unfairness for the sake of the greater good.

QALYs belong to the realm of maximizing. They cannot be used to determine everything about the distribution of resources. But neither

---

[9] Need is one of the most plausible sources of claims. See David Wiggins, 'Claims of Need', in Ted Honderich (ed.), *Morality and Objectivity* (London: Routledge and Kegan Paul, 1985). Michael Lockwood argues from the supposition that claims are proportional to need in his contribution to this volume. Lockwood's argument has a lot in common with mine, but I disagree with his suggestion that weaker claims may justly be overridden by stronger ones.

[10] There is brief discussion of these two sorts of utilitarian in my paper, op. cit.

can they be condemned as worthless because they take no account of fairness.

V

The QALYs produced by a treatment, then, are supposed to measure how beneficial the treatment is, how much good it leads to. How well do they do that? I shall start to answer this question by taking a small part of it. The QALYs a treatment brings a particular person are supposed to measure the good the treatment does her. How well do they do that?

Underlying the use of QALYs to measure a person's good are two assumptions. The first is that her good is the total of the good that comes to her at all times in her life. The second is that the goodness of her life at each time is determined but its 'quality', as reflected in the 'quality adjustment factor' embedded in a QALY. I shall say something about these in turn.

There are many rivals to the assumption that a person's good can be found by adding across time. First, there is the view that when good is aggregated across time it is not necessarily right to do it just by adding. For instance, it might be good to have a life in which good is evenly spread across time, so it is worth accepting a reduction in the total of good for the sake of evenness. Or perhaps a good life is one that ends well. Another rival view is that there are goods that cannot be assigned to any particular time at all. For instance, there is the good of making a success of your life. These rival views are, I think, serious objections to the idea that a person's good is given by adding across time. I have not yet formed an opinion about them.

A very important implication of this idea is that there is no question of incommensurability between length of life and quality of life. If a person's life is extended, this idea implies that the good done her is no more or less than the extra good she enjoys during the extended lifetime. The good of extending a life is not a different sort of good from the goods that are enjoyed during a life. This seems exactly right to me, but again I am not going to argue for it here.

The second assumption is that the goodness of a life at a time is determined by its 'quality'. What in practice is meant by quality is a state of health such as: confined to a wheelchair and in slight pain. Each quality is assigned an adjustment factor. Perfect health has a factor of one; other states of health have smaller factors. If, say, some state has a factor of a half, that means it is supposed to be half as good as being in good health. This in turn means that to live two years in this state is supposed to be exactly as good for a person as to live one year in good health.

John Broome

The first comment to make about this is that there are obviously lots of things besides her health that affect how good a person's life is at a time. There is her wealth, for instance. When we are talking about a single patient, the way to deal with this point is simply to suppose that all the other things are kept constant. Then we need only worry about health. But actually different people's QALYs are going to be put together and added up. To do so assumes implicitly that a QALY to one person represents just as much good as a QALY to another. And that is plainly false. Some people have much better lives than others in the same state of health.

Good is better promoted by extending good lives rather than less good ones. It is a weakness in QALYs as a measure of good that they ignore many aspects of good. Possibly, it may not be a practically important weakness, because it may be that on the large scale where QALYs are used, in the general allocation of resources, differences in the goodness of lives will cancel each other out. But actually I doubt it. Many diseases are fairly specific to economic classes, or regions of the country, or races. This means there must be some systematic connections between diseases and the goodness of the lives of their victims.

A natural response to this point is to say that it is right to ignore these facts about the goodness of people's lives. Just because one person has a better life than another—say she has a job and lives in a comfortable suburb—that does not mean she better deserves to have her life extended. It is a *merit* of QALYs that they take no account of these things. But this is a mistake. The reason it is wrong to give priority to the person with a better life is that it is unfair to do so. Fairness is not the business of QALYs. Suppose one person has a better life than another, but this time because she has better health. QALY calculations will unblushingly count the former person as more worth saving. This is correct as far as it goes: more good is done by saving a good life than a bad one. And it is just as correct if the cause is economic privilege as it is if the cause is good health. Fairness pulls in the other direction, but that is a separate consideration.

Suppose, though, that the quality adjustment factor is going to be determined from the state of health only. How can it be properly determined? How do we settle whether or not some state is half as good as good health? Various methods are used in practice to determine these factors. The commonest in principle is to base them on people's preferences in some way. So one state, say, is counted as half as good as good health if people are indifferent between living for two years in that state and living one year in good health. But there are theoretical and practical difficulties. I have examined them more thoroughly in another paper,[11] and I shall skip over them now.

[11] John Broome, 'Notes on qalys', in Michael Banner and Basil Mitchell (eds), *Ian Ramsey Centre Report Number 2* (Blackwell, forthcoming).

VI

Now let us leave all these questions aside, and suppose that a person's good is indeed the total of her QALYs. Granted this, is the benefit of a treatment the total of the QALYs it produces for everyone? To put it another way, is good the total of the good of individuals? To rely on the total of QALYs in distributing resources supposes that it is.

Utilitarians believe that good is the total of people's good. So amongst the objections to this claim will be some of the usual objections to utilitarianism. Not all of the usual objections, however. Some of them are objections to different utilitarian claims, such as the claim that the right way to act is always to maximize good. This is not now in question. Remember, too, that I have restricted 'good' to good excluding fairness, so the usual objections to utilitarianism on grounds of fairness will not be relevant.

One objection that may be relevant suggests that for a given total of good it is better to have it more evenly distributed between people than less evenly. So good is not just the total of people's good. I am puzzled by this suggestion, and I have examined it quite carefully in another article.[12] Here I shall simply say that the motivation behind it is presumably a concern for fairness, and I hope I have already dealt with that.

Another objection is that there may be sorts of good that are not people's good at all. The good of animals is a possible example, and so is the variety of natural species. But I cannot think of any examples that are likely to be significant in distributing health resources. So I shall leave this objection aside.

The objections I shall be concerned with are ones that come up within the fold of utilitarianism, rather than from outside. They are questions that have worried utilitarians when issues arise about changing the population of the world. They are also important when it comes to lengthening people's lives, for instance by medicine. They are, I think, much the most serious problems with the idea of allocating health resources on the basis of QALYs.

There are two ways of increasing the number of QALYs. One is to improve or extend the lives of existing people. The other is to bring new people into the world. Many medical decisions, and decisions about the distribution of resources in medicine, are very directly about the latter. There are decisions about the treatment of infertility, antenatal care, saving the lives of pregnant women, contraception and so on. And a great many other medical decisions affect the creation of new people

[12] John Broome, 'Utilitarianism and Expected Utility', *Journal of Philosophy* **84** (1987).

less directly. Whenever a young person's life is saved there is a good chance she will later have children who would otherwise never have existed. The practitioners of QALY calculations need to take a view on whether or not they should count the QALYs of new people. In practice, I believe they have never counted them. I shall call this the 'standard practice': in assessing the benefit of an act do not count the QALYs of people who come into existence as a result of it. Is the standard practice right or wrong?

Some utilitarians would think it is wrong. 'Classical' utilitarians[13] believe that good is simply the total of people's good, irrespective of whom it belongs to. So they count the good of new people equally with the good of existing people. But classical utilitarianism has problems of its own. For one thing it has many implausible consequences. Derek Parfit's 'repugnant conclusion' is one.[14] Another is that it makes it hard to be in favour both of prolonging the lives of existing people and reducing the number of people who are born. Making babies is doubtless a cheaper way of generating QALYs than saving lives.

Besides, other utilitarians would give their support to this aspect of QALY calculations. Jan Narveson[15] argues that the benefit of an act is the good it brings to existing people (and people who will exist anyway, whether or not the act is done), but does not include the good of people who come into existence as a result of the act. His argument can be put like this. The benefits of an act consist of the benefits it brings to people. But bringing a person into existence does not benefit her, however good her life may be. To benefit a person you have to make her better off than she would otherwise have been, and it cannot be true of a person who would otherwise not have existed at all that she is better off than she would otherwise have been.

VII

So it would be wrong to dismiss the standard practice straightaway. But now think about an example: the question of dividing resources between maternity hospitals where they will save the lives of newborn babies, and other hospitals where they will save the lives of adults. Imagine, in fact, that there is a particular choice between saving a baby and saving a twenty-year-old. And suppose that if the baby dies her

[13] Such as Henry Sidgwick, *The Methods of Ethics* (London: Macmillan, 1907).

[14] Derek Parfit, *Reasons and Persons* (Oxford University Press, 1984), Part IV.

[15] 'Utilitarianism and New Generations', *Mind* **76** (1967), 62–72.

parents will soon have another baby instead. According to the view I am describing, it is better to save the baby. That will give her, say, eighty QALYs. Saving the twenty-year-old will give her sixty. The good of the baby's possible replacement does not come into this calculation at all.

I think this conclusion is intuitively unattractive. It makes a great deal out of the difference between the baby and the replacement, the fact that one exists and the other does not. Suppose the moment of decision in the example is pushed back in time, to before the baby is born, or before she becomes implanted in the womb, or before she is conceived. It will have to be settled where along this sequence the baby exists and where she does not. The moment when she comes into existence makes all the difference to the QALY calculation. After it, all the QALYs in the whole of her life get taken into account; before it, none. Since the beginning of a person seems inherently vague, it seems implausible that such a lot should turn on the moment when it happens.[16]

This is a difficulty with the standard practice. But I think it can be overcome. I shall start by pinpointing what I think is the source of the problem. The standard practice puts a tremendous weight on the fact of a person's continuing identity through her life. In the example, the baby's QALYs get counted as a benefit of saving her, even the ones that will come to her when she is in her seventies, because she will then still be the same person as the baby now living. Her replacement, however, when she gets to her seventies, will not be the same person as this baby. Therefore her QALYs are not counted. It is implausible, I think, that this fact of transtemporal identity should make such a difference so far in the future.

Derek Parfit's theory of personal identity[17] offers grounds for attaching less weight to the fact of identity. I, now, am the same as the old person I shall become if I live that long. But Parfit argues that what has importance in moral questions is not actually my identity with this old person, but the psychological connections between us. He includes particularly connections of memory. The connections need not be direct. The old person may perhaps remember nothing I do now. But in a few years I shall remember some of what I do now, and a few years after that I shall remember some of the things I did a few years earlier, and so on. There will be an overlapping chain of memories running from me now to the old person. Parfit counts that as a connection. He also includes other psychological connections besides memory. There are intentions, for instance. In a few years I shall carry out some of the

---

[16] Helge Kuhse and Peter Singer, in an unpublished paper 'The Economic Assessment of Neo-natal Intensive Care: Some Problems' make this point.
[17] Op. cit. Part III.

intentions I have now, and a few years after that I shall carry out some of the intentions I had a few years earlier, and so on along a chain to the old person.

According to Parfit, it is these psychological connections that make it the case that I am the same as that old person. Consequently the moral importance that actually attaches to the connections can easily look as though it attaches to the identity. But this is a mistake; it is the connections that matter. The connections between moments in a person's life will generally be weaker the further apart they are in time. And if they are weaker it may be that they have less moral importance.

A baby is very weakly connected psychologically with the rest of her life. So perhaps we should not attach much importance to the connection. But the standard practice attaches a lot of importance to it. Perhaps the standard practice should be modified.

How? In the example the standard practice counted all the QALYs of the baby but none of the QALYs of the replacement, on grounds of transtemporal identity. Now we see that such a large difference in treatment may not be justified when the psychological connections are weak. So we should either start counting the replacement's QALYs, or count the baby's less. To start counting the replacement's would be to abandon the basic principle of the standard practice. So let us pursue the alternative of counting the baby's less. This suggests *discounting* the future QALYs because of the weakening of the psychological connections that carry moral significance. It implies that the baby's QALYs should be very drastically discounted, because the connections are so weak.

I think this gives an intuitively attractive solution to the problem about the baby. It says it would almost certainly be better to save the twenty-year-old than the baby. And nothing now depends on a precise determination of the moment when a person comes into existence. As we go back earlier in the baby's life, the psychological connections with the rest of her life will fade away to nothing.

The discounting I am suggesting works in a complicated way.[18] Suppose we are facing a decision between two alternative acts. Take first the people who will exist if we pick one of the alternatives but not the other. The good of these people is not to be counted in making the decision. That is the principle we are working on: not to count the good of people whose existence results from our act. Now take the people who will exist in either alternative. If they have the same lifetime in each, we count all of their good in both. But take a person (P) who lives a longer time in one than in the other. During the time when P is alive in

[18] It is spelled out more fully in John Broome, 'The Economic Value of Life', *Economics* **52** (1984), 281–294.

one alternative but not in the other, the only morally significant fact that distinguishes her from somebody (Q) who is alive in the one but never exists at all in the other is that P is psychologically connected with herself at a time when she exists in both. The weaker the connection, the less significant is the fact. Since we do not count Q's QALYs at all, we should discount P's QALYs according to the weakness of the connection. This means discounting the QALYs a person enjoys at times when she is alive in only one of the alternatives, and discounting them according to the difference between their date and the nearest date when she is alive in both.

This is not at all like the discounting that is commonly adopted by economists in calculations about QALYs. Economists generally give less weight to QALYs that occur further in the future.[19] The discount is determined simply by the date when the QALY comes. Good that comes later is counted as less valuable than good that comes earlier, simply because it comes later. I do not think this can be justified. But it is too complicated a subject to take up here.

To see the difference between the two sorts of discounting, think about the question of how much to spend on clearing up asbestos. Asbestos takes a long time to kill people. So the benefit of clearing it up is that some people who would have died in, say, forty years will not die for fifty. Take a person who gains, then, ten QALYs starting in forty years' time. Discounting in the conventional way will make these QALYs count for very little, because they will be discounted by at least forty years. Discounting my way discounts them by at most ten.

VIII

I have tried out one objection on the standard practice, and suggested a way it might be warded off. But there are more serious objections to come.

The basic principle of the standard practice is to count as a benefit of an action the good of existing people and people who will exist anyway, but not the good of people who come into existence as a result of the action itself. I mentioned that this principle has been supported by Jan Narveson. However, it runs into so many severe difficulties that it really seems impossible to sustain it in the end. This case is, I think, conclusively made by Derek Parfit.[20] Here I shall only mention two of the difficulties.

[19] See, for instance, Alan Williams, 'Economics of Coronary Artery Bypass Grafting', *British Medical Journal* **291** (1985), 326–329.
[20] Op. cit. Part IV.

John Broome

The first is that the class of 'people who come into existence as a result of the action itself' is only defined relative to what the alternative actions are. If the choice is between A and B, the principle says that the only good that should count in this choice is the good of people who will exist whichever of A or B is chosen. If the choice is between B and C, it is only the good of people who will exist whichever of B or C is chosen. If the choice is between C and A, only the good of people who will exist whichever of C or A is chosen. These may be different groups of people each time. Consequently an intransitivity may arise. The principle may conclude that A is better than B, B than C, and C than A. This is a contradiction.

The second difficulty is what Parfit calls 'the identity objection'. Many medical decisions affect who comes into existence. In fact, most do so indirectly, since they affect who meets whom and marries, when they have children and so on. Some do so more directly. Suppose a technique becomes available that prevents genetically defective people from being conceived, by disabling defective sperms and ova. Already some selection is possible in *in vitro* fertilization. This technique would ensure that different, healthy people come into existence instead of the unhealthy people who otherwise would have.

What benefit would this technique have? According to the standard practice it would have none. If the technique is applied, the healthy people who come into existence would not otherwise have existed at all. So their QALYs do not count as a benefit of the technique. This is absurd. To be sure, there may be reasons for doubting that the technique would be beneficial all things considered. There are serious worries about the long-term effects of this sort of eugenics. Its risks might outweigh its benefits. But to suggest it has no benefits at all is absurd. Besides, I only picked this example because the effect of the technique on the identity of the people who come into existence is so direct. Even with a decision that affects identities more indirectly, the same difficulty will arise.

Because of these difficulties and others, I believe that the standard practice in QALY calculations is ultimately indefensible.

What alternative is there? There is the classical utilitarian view, which counts as the benefit of an act all the good received by everyone, whether or not the act brings them into existence. This overcomes the problems I have just mentioned. But classical utilitarianism has serious problems of its own—I mentioned some earlier—and is not really an acceptable alternative. The trouble is that no acceptable alternative is available. This is the negative conclusion that comes out of Parfit's extensive investigation of population theory.[21]

---

[21] Ibid.

IX

Perhaps an acceptable alternative will emerge. In the meantime my conclusion can only be negative too. The use of QALYs is, I think, a valuable attempt to assess good in medical contexts. It does not take account of fairness. But it should not be blamed for that, so long as it is recognized that fairness also matters. It has some difficulties that can be overcome. But it also has some difficulties that cannot be overcome and, when pressed, these seem to be fatal.[22]

[22] I have had some very useful discussion with Michael Lockwood on the subject of this paper.

More and Better Justice

JOHN HARRIS

I. The Equality Principle

The principle that people's lives and fundamental interests are of equal value and that they must therefore be given equal weight has immense intellectual appeal and intuitive force. It is often enough to discredit a theory or proposal simply to show that it violates this principle. When measures are said to be discriminatory or unfair it is this principle which is in play. Recent philosophers of widely differing schools and outlooks give versions of this principle a central role in their theories.

Ronald Dworkin for example gives it a central and fundamental place when he makes it part of our understanding of the point of taking rights seriously. He suggests that:

> Anyone who professes to take rights seriously . . . must accept at the minimum one or both of two important ideas. The first is the vague but powerful idea of human dignity. This idea, associated with Kant but defended by philosophers of different schools, supposes that there are ways of treating a man that are inconsistent with recognizing him as a full member of the human community, and holds that such treatment is profoundly unjust.
>
> The second is the more familiar idea of political equality. This supposes that the weaker members of a political community are entitled to the same concern and respect of their government as the more powerful members have secured for themselves . . .
>
> It makes sense to say that a man has a fundamental right against the Government, in the strong sense, like free speech, if that right is necessary to protect his dignity, or his standing as equally entitled to concern and respect or some other personal value of like consequence. It does not make sense otherwise.[1]

Interestingly, Dworkin also argues that it is this principle that lies at the heart of John Rawls' famous account of justice when he concludes that 'justice as fairness rests on the assumption of a natural right of all men and women to equality of concern and respect . . .'[2]

---

[1] Ronald Dworkin, *Taking Rights Seriously* (London: Duckworth, 1977), 198.
[2] Ibid. 182.

From a very different perspective, Robert Nozick, in arguing against the legitimacy of using or sacrificing some people for the sake of others, suggests that 'a state or government that claims . . . [the citizen's] allegiance . . . therefore scrupulously must be *neutral* between its citizens'.[3]

Recently, Jonathan Glover has made interesting use of a version of this principle.[4] He extends it to cover our obligations to future generations suggesting that what he calls 'the equality principle' states 'that people's interests should be given equal weight regardless of their generation'.[5] Having reviewed the theoretical superstructure provided for this basic principle by R. M. Hare and John Rawls, Glover goes on to argue that this principle 'can be supported by reasons which do not require any such theoretical superstructure'.[6] He illustrates the intuitive appeal of the principle with a parable provided by R. and V. Routley[7] which they produce to illustrate the obligations created by nuclear power. They ask us to consider a bus journey:

> The bus carries both passengers and freight on its long journey. It is always crowded but passengers keep getting on and off, and the drivers change so that quite different people are on board at different stages of the journey. Early in the journey, a container of highly toxic and explosive gas is put aboard, destined for somewhere near the end of the route. The container is very thin, and the consignor knows it is unlikely to survive the journey intact. If it breaks, some of the passengers will probably be killed. Sending the container of gas on the bus seems an appalling act. The consignor might make various excuses. It is not *certain* the gas will escape. If it does, perhaps the bus will have crashed and killed everyone first. . . . He further tries to justify his act by pleading economic necessity: his business will crash unless he sends the container on the bus.[8]

Glover endorses the Routley's claim that none of this adds up to a good defence of the consignor's actions and goes on to consider and reject one further point that might be made. 'That is that the harm done does not matter at all, simply because it happens to people who are not on the bus at the time the container is put aboard'.[9] He points out, surely rightly,

[3] Robert Nozick, *Anarchy State and Utopia* (Oxford: Blackwell, 1974), 33.

[4] Jonathan Glover, *What Sort of People Should There Be?* (Harmondsworth: Penguin, 1984), 40–42.

[5] Ibid. 140.

[6] Ibid. 142.

[7] R. and V. Routley paraphrased by Glover, ibid. 142, from their 'Nuclear Energy And Obligations to the Future', *Inquiry* (1978).

[8] Ibid.

[9] Ibid.

that we are no more justified in killing future people than present people; and he might well have added that the consignor's action would not be thought significantly more acceptable if the bus carried only kindergarten children or for that matter old people. Glover concludes his discussion of this point by noting that 'people's moral claims are not reduced by when they live, any more than they are by where they live. And that is the equality principle.'[10]

Had Glover's interest not been primarily in moral claims between generations, he might have added that people's moral claims are not reduced by who they are, or how old they are or by how rich or poor, powerful or weak they are. The equality principle covers young and old, present and future people and may be taken as stating that people's lives and fundamental interests should be given equal weight regardless of race, creed, colour, gender and age, economic status and regardless of their generation.

The equality principle is not only, as I have suggested, widely accepted, it is also widely believed to be both part of the morality and part of the political philosophy of most Western societies. This of course does not mean that there are not huge differences about how this principle is to be interpreted. In part, what follows is an argument about just this. However, the principle is, I want to suggest, sufficiently widely held, and sufficiently respected and respectable, to shift the onus of justification on to those who wish to defend breaches of it or departures from it.

It has recently been suggested that the equality principle is mistaken or misunderstood and that in particular people's moral claims might be reduced by how old they are and by their quality of life and by how much keeping them alive costs the rest of us: by the quality or quantity either of the life they have lived or the life they expect to live, or by the quantity of money it will cost for them to live it. It is this suggestion that I wish to examine in what follows.

II. QALYs

The Quality Adjusted Life Year or QALY[11] has been invented to perform a number of very useful tasks in health care. It is supposedly a criterion of beneficial health care, a measure of efficiency in health care, and a method of settling priorities in health care. If it can perform all these functions without harmful side effects it will indeed be one of the most significant advances in health care since the water closet.

[10] Ibid. 144.
[11] George Teeling Smith, Office of Health Economics, *The Measurement of Health* (London, 1985).

At the risk of repeating what is said elsewhere in this volume, let me just make clear precisely what the QALY is, according to its inventor.

> The essence of a QALY is that it takes a year of healthy life expectancy to be worth 1, but regards a year of unhealthy life expectancy as worth less than 1. Its precise value is lower the worse the quality of life of the unhealthy person (which is what the 'quality adjusted' bit is all about). If being dead is worth zero, it is, in principle, possible for a QALY to be negative, i.e. for the quality of someone's life to be judged worse than being dead.
>
> The general idea is that a beneficial health care activity is one that generates a positive amount of QALYs, and that an efficient health care activity is one where the cost per QALY is as low as it can be. A high priority health care activity is one where the cost-per-QALY is low, and a low priority activity is one where cost-per-QALY is high.[12]

The plausibility of the QALY derives from the idea that 'given the choice', a person would prefer a shorter healthier life to a longer period of survival in a state of severe discomfort and disability.[13] The idea that any rational person would endorse this preference provides the moral and political force behind the QALY. Its acceptability as a measurement of health then depends upon its doing all the theoretical tasks assigned to it, and on its being what people want, or would want, for themselves.

I have set out in detail elsewhere[14] what I believe to be the many problems with and objections to QALYs. My present concern is with just one set of their side effects. These concern the way in which they operate to reduce people's moral claims to the protection of the equality principle, and the sorts of arguments that might be adduced to justify this side effect or to demonstrate that it is apparent rather than real.

QALYs are so versatile that their inventors believe firmly that they do not have the problems associated with them to which we have just alluded.

Williams suggests that QALYs involve the idea that 'one year of healthy life is of equal value no matter who gets it', and that each person's valuations 'have equal weight'.[15] He clearly believes that this

[12] Alan Williams, 'The Value of QALYs', *Health and Social Service Journal* (18 July 1985), '*Centre Eight*', 3.

[13] Teeling Smith, op. cit. 16.

[14] See my 'QALYfying the Value of Life', in *Journal of Medical Ethics* **13**, No. 3 (September 1987), and my 'EQALYty', in P. Byrne (ed.), *King's College Studies* (forthcoming).

[15] Alan Williams, op. cit., 5.

constitutes all the moral defence that QALYs need and that it brings them under the protection of the equality principle. Now this is clearly false, but some dimensions of its falsehood are easily demonstrated, other parts have more initial plausibility. We will start with the easy bits.

There are two dimensions to the most obviously discriminatory features of QALYs and they have to do with what I will call the 'ageist' feature of the QALY measurement.

Time is What Counts

The first is that it establishes life units, in this case life-years, as the entities which have value and which are to be maximized. On this view it is not people who are valuable, it is not people who are to be protected by the equality principle, but simply units of lifetime. This is an interesting idea, because if it is right then what matters in life is how many life units the world contains—it doesn't matter whose they are. On this view it is a matter of moral indifference whether thirty people live for one year more or that one person lives for thirty years more. Moreover, so long as people are replaced on a one for one (or a better than one for one) basis, it doesn't matter whether individuals live or die. From the life-units perspective the world is as well endowed as it was before—or better!

It is true that advocates of QALYs have not exactly emphasized this feature of QALYs. They prefer to see the idea in terms of giving actual people more of what they want.

Now this will happen if QALYs are only used as a method of choosing between therapies for given candidates. If I can be treated either this way or that, and that offers me more QALYs, I'd be a fool not to take it. The problem arises however because QALYs are designed more to help officials—from doctors, through health authorities right up to governments—than they are to help patients. And in this role they operate with a distinctly ageist basis.

Ageism

The ageism of QALY is inescapable, for any calculation of the life-years generated for a particular patient by a particular therapy must be based on the life expectancy of that patient after treatment. The older the patient is when treated, the fewer the life-years that can be achieved by the therapy.

It is true that QALYs dictate that we prefer not simply those who have *more life expectancy* but rather those who have *more life expectancy to be gained from treatment*. But wherever treatment helps postpone death, and this will be frequently (for quite simple treatments like a timely antibiotic can be life saving), it will, other things being equal, be the case that younger people have more life expectancy to gain from treatment than do older people.

So if QALYs encapsulate a moral imperative which requires that one year is of equal value no matter who gets it, then it follows that:

> (a) It is a matter of moral indifference that one person gets thirty or that six people get five each or that thirty get one each,

and

> (b) That it will usually be more QALY efficient to concentrate on areas of medicine which will inevitably generate more QALYs, neonatal care or paediatrics for example. And equally, to channel resources away from (or deny them altogether to) areas such as geriatric medicine or terminal care,

and

> (c) That this may sometimes mean people receiving trivial amounts of quality adjusted time at the expense of significant amounts for (fewer) others. It's worth just spelling out why this is so.

The Problem of Short Remission

It is always assumed that QALYs will operate to favour longer periods of survival for fewer patients over shorter periods for greater numbers—hence it's ageism. This will often be the case and where it is, QALYs will indeed be ageist. Indeed critics of QALYs are often castigated for defending the equality principle because this might lead to old people being preferred to younger ones when they can only survive for relatively short periods. But QALYs can also have this effect. Suppose that the same resources could purchase a treatment which would prolong the lives of 121,000 people by one month but could alternatively give ten more years of life each to 1,000 people. If one unit of lifespan is of equal value no matter who gets it then the 121,000 life months available from the first alternative are morally preferable to the mere 120,000 life months which giving 1000 individuals ten more years of life each would provide. Nothing in the moral theory of QALYs nor I think in the economic theory either, is able to cope with possibilities like this. Whether defenders of QALYs are content with such possibilities is of course for them to say.[16]

[16] See my *The Value of Life: An Introduction to Medical Ethics* (London: Routledge & Kegan Paul, 1985), 96ff. These problems and possible solutions are more fully discussed there.

Economism

Money also counts. Because a high priority health care activity is one where the cost per QALY is low and a low priority activity is one where the cost per QALY is high, QALYs require us to be frugal as well as ageist. We must not only choose the treatment which will generate the most life-years, we must also choose the treatment which is cheapest. And not only the treatment either. QALYs demand that we choose the *illness* or condition that is cheapest to treat! This may lead us to ignore diseases or conditions which are expensive to treat, even though as experience is gained the price may well be reduced, even though there might be much to learn in the process and even if, though the price of treating each individual be high, relatively few people are involved and so the total cost is in fact small. The effect of this might be to deny people afflicted in a certain way any hope at all—simply to write them off and thus ignore their moral claims to society's concern and respect, so denying them the protection of the equality principle. I shall call this idea that individuals be denied the protection of the equality principle for economic reasons, 'economism'.

Economism and the Equality Principle

At first sight it might seem not only sensible but also consistent with the equality principle to ensure that 'as much benefit as possible is obtained from resources devoted to health care'[17] where these resources are public resources. However, Dworkin is surely right to identify the notion of political equality with the idea that 'weaker members of a political community are entitled to the same concern and respect of their government as the more powerful members have secured for themselves'. Now the poor are of course paradigms of the weak that Dworkin had in mind, and one central requirement, if they are to be shown equal concern and respect, is to ensure that by one means or another they have access to adequate health care. But this access would be limited indeed if the proviso was added that they could have access to health care only on condition that they did not suffer from anything that was expensive to treat. This would be to introduce proper health care only for the rich by another route. Indeed, if the care could only be provided by a public health service, it might also introduce a new class of the poor (and hence weak). Not those with little money but those with expensive diseases or conditions.

It must be remembered that the point of ensuring that the poor have access to health care is not because the poor are specially deserving,

---

[17] Alan Williams, 'Economics of Coronary Artery Bypass Grafting', *British Medical Journal* **291** (3 August 1985), 326.

rather it is that because their lives matter as much as anyone else's, the equality principle demands that they have equal access to life-preserving and life-enhancing health care. To give low priority to those with conditions that are expensive to treat is to make the value of life turn on the cost of preserving it.

III. Defending QALYs

(a) Modest Defences

There are modest and immodest defences that might be made to the charge that QALYs violate the equality principle. The modest ones are modest indeed but we must deal briefly with them. There are two such defences and they both have to do with the interpretation of QALYs as ageist and economist.

The first defence is that QALYs so far from operating to recommend treatment only or primarily of conditions that affect the young or younger members of society, rather they notoriously advocate the treatment of conditions which do in fact affect the old. The example always cited in this context[18] is that of QALYs noted preference for hip replacement operations (which benefit mainly old people) rather than coronary artery bypass grafting. In a well-known paper Alan Williams discusses the economics of coronary artery bypass grafting and compares such operations adversely with, *inter alia*, hip replacement operations.[19] It is true that this is what Williams does in that paper. But he also states in the same place and very firmly that 'Coronary artery bypass grafting is one of many contenders for additional resources'. Ideally, all such contenders should be compared each time a decision on allocation of resources is made to test which should be cut back and which should be expanded.[20] If this is done it is unlikely that hip replacement operations would get a look in, for their proper peer group would not simply be the QALY inefficient coronary bypass grafts but, *inter alia*, the ultraefficient GP advice to stop smoking which generates 1,197 QALYs per £200,000 invested as opposed to a mere 266 for hip replacements.[21]

The second modest defence is that QALYs are intended to operate only at the margin where contenders for *additional* resources are examined.[22] Why this should be so is unclear. Either QALYs are the

[18] And I have heard Alan Williams and Alan Maynard do so on a number of occasions, though not so far as I am aware in print.

[19] Alan Williams, op. cit.

[20] Ibid. 326.

[21] BBC TV, *The Heart of the Matter,* (October 1986).

[22] Alan Williams, op. cit. 326, 329. Again I have heard Williams and Maynard say this in discussion.

right method of resource allocation or they are not. If they are right then they should clearly operate across the board. If they are not right we should be protected from them even at the margin.

(b) Immodest Defences

The immodest defence of QALYs must attempt to show that its moral costs are outweighed by its moral benefits.

The moral force behind QALYs is threefold. There is the idea that scarce resources should purchase as much benefit as is possible. There is the idea that what is purchased be perceived as a benefit (hence the quality adjustment) and there is the idea that the QALY is impartial, valuing an adjusted year equally irrespective of who gets it.

The first two moral claims made for QALYs have some force but they do not operate against the objections standardly made here and elsewhere against QALYs.[23]

I have no objections to the idea that benefits should be perceived as such and that quality of survival is as important as survival rates. And of course scarce resources should purchase as much benefit as possible. As I have suggested at length elsewhere,[24] where individuals use them to decide which of rival therapies are best for them, QALYs are benign and useful. However, the crucial issue turns on an understanding of what it is to obtain maximum benefit from resources. The resources it must be remembered are public resources and we expect and require that these resources be used to purchase maximum benefit for the public—that is for society as a whole. This will be achieved if they are used in ways that do not violate the equality principle—in short, if everyone is treated impartially in their distribution. So the whole burden of the defence of QALYs comes down to whether or not they operate impartially. Unless of course it is argued that we ought not to be impartial in the distribution of health care resources. However, since none of the defenders of QALYs have suggested this I shall ignore it at this time.

IV. Impartiality

There is a powerful *prima facie* case against QALYs. We have shown how they inevitably operate to discriminate against those who are old or

---

[23] See the papers in note 14 above and John Grimley Evans, 'The Sanctity of Life', in John Elford (ed.), *Medical Ethics and Elderly People* (Edinburgh: Churchill Livingstone, 1987).

[24] See note 14 above.

have less life-expectancy than others and against those who are expensive to treat. That is, they are what I have called ageist and economist. They also incidentally can operate against some racial groups and against accident victims in ways that raise questions of double jeopardy. I have shown how this works elsewhere and the points though not insignificant are peripheral to the argument so I will not press them again here.[25]

Williams clearly believes that QALYs are impartial on the face of it and that his claim that with QALYs 'one year of healthy life is of equal value no matter who gets it' is some sort of guarantee of this. However, if it doesn't matter who gets it then it doesn't matter that one person collars the lot. From the QALY perspective it is a matter of indifference whether one person gets forty years or forty people get one each, both scenarios satisfy the requirement that one year is of equal value no matter who gets it. However, QALYs may have better claims to impartiality than Williams and others have given them credit for and I'd like to consider two defences that might be made of QALY impartiality.

QALYs and Impartiality

It might be claimed simply that QALYs are impartial on the face of it. They are blind to race, creed, colour, gender, nationality and so on, and despite their ageist *consequences* they do not mention age at all and may, in some circumstances, actually benefit even the old. It may be that some major ethical theory impartially couched (perhaps some versions of utilitarianism) would support them and if so then the claim that they are discriminatory looks weak or weaker.[26] Certainly the designers of QALYs do not believe or wish them to be discriminatory and have indeed designed them impartially. However, even measures designed to operate impartially on the face of it and supported by major ethical theories impartially couched, may *in fact* operate in a discriminatory fashion.

Take as a parallel, college admissions systems or job or professional admissions systems which, because perhaps they admit only those with the highest qualifications and thus give equal weight to equal qualifications regardless of who gets the qualifications, regardless of race, colour, creed, gender, etc., are impartial on the face of it and so will apparently be supported by any major ethical theories that have impartiality or equality at their core. It is, however, now notorious that such systems can and do operate to perpetuate and reinforce discrimination

[25] Ibid.

[26] I owe this suggestion to Peter Singer who has helped me to clarify many of the issues in this paper.

against some racial groups and women in some circumstances; and that they do so despite the best will on the part of those who design and administer them. When this happens these impartial systems simply serve to perpetuate impacted advantage and disadvantage and so operate in a way which violates and undermines the very values it apparently enshrines and which are its major legitimation.

Such effects may well not be apparent when the system is considered in the abstract. We need to see or imagine how it will operate in fact. I have argued that QALYs will inevitably operate to discriminate against the old, those with less life expectancy than others, and those with conditions that are expensive to treat. If this is right then all the *prima facie* impartiality in the world should not blind us to their *de facto* discriminatory consequences.

This is not of course my view alone. John Grimley Evans (Professor of Geriatric Medicine, University of Oxford) has written:

> Modern egalitarianism, in which we justify contemporary British civilization, recognizes all individuals as equal. It does not accept that some are less equal because they are female or black, biological characteristics over which the individual . . . [has] . . . no personal control, and age is another biological characteristic meriting similar status. If pressed, proponents of the lost life-years approach to priorities in medicine are forced to confess that their underlying assumption relates to the economic worth of lives of working age, the value in other words of an individual's work to the State. This approach is fundamentally Fascist, using this much misused term in its essential sense of subordination of the individual to the purpose of the State . . .[27]

Similarly, Alwyn Smith (Professor of Epidemiology and Social Oncology, University of Manchester) notes:

> In . . . terms . . . [of QALYs] the value for money associated with geriatric medicine—and especially with the care of the dying— would inevitably be low.[28]

The conclusion is, I think, inescapable that however impartially the theory of QALYs has been expressed, and however it is designed, it will be discriminatory in fact.

QALYs and Equality

It might be suggested that, despite its discriminatory tendencies, my rejection of QALYs depends on a mistaken or tendentious interpreta-

[27] John Grimley Evans, op. cit.
[28] Alwyn Smith, *Qualms About QALYs,* unpublished MS., Manchester University, 1986.

John Harris

tion of the equality principle. In terms of health care the equality principle demands that each person be given an equal chance of benefiting from health care, and that I have given insufficient attention to what might sensibly be meant by 'benefiting'.[29] The idea here must be that people would trade off the chance of a shorter period of remission (fewer QALYs) in some circumstances for the opportunity of a longer period of remission (more QALYs) in another. This they would regard as obtaining an equal chance of benefiting with the accent on a particular view of what it is to benefit.

An immediate response might be that here as in so many other areas, it is one thing to opt for such a trade-off for oneself, quite another to impose it on others against their will even if those others constitute a minority. QALYs, it must be noted, will inevitably operate not at the point of sale, so to speak, but will be imposed by doctors or more likely by hospital or health authority administrators or by government. However, if each person gets an equal chance of benefiting and if many or even most would regard this as a desirable trade-off, then why not?

To see more clearly why not let's try to put QALYs in an even better light and look more closely at this question.

V. Consent

Actual Consent

In an interesting and sympathetic consideration of QALYs, Paul Menzel has discussed the point at hand.[30] He makes the moral case for QALYs rest on the issue of consent and states his point thus:

> The moral case for QALYs rests heavily on the claim that it is people themselves who quality rank their own lives. If this claim is true, QALYs should elicit no images whatsoever of Nazi euthanasia program judgments by some people about others' inferior quality of life. They will represent only people's own judgments about how they would allocate resources to lives of different quality.[31]

Menzel goes on to point out that people are willing to trade-off, or 'gamble' chances of death against chances of recovery when they accept medical treatment and he then notes:

> There is . . . an important conceptual connexion between . . . willingness to gamble and the long-term societal use of QALYs. If I

[29] Here also I am indebted to Peter Singer.
[30] Paul T. Menzel, *Creepy QALYs,* unpublished MS., Department of Philosophy, Pacific Lutheran University, Tacoma, WA 98447, USA.
[31] Ibid. 6.

now endorse them as an allocation principle, what do they involve for me and my life? They expose me to a greater risk of being allowed to die if I should ever be . . . [a] paraplegic accident victim, but in return I gain a better chance of being saved should I ever be a victim with prospectively normal health. Let's call this the 'QALY bargain'. If, knowing full well what a particular state of illness is like, I am willing to take the standard gamble—a ten per cent risk of dying, say, in order to restore myself to good health—wouldn't I also likely be willing to take the QALY bargain?[32]

If this is right then Menzel believes that only technical problems remain. They are to ask the right questions of the sample used by QALY researchers to obtain the quality values for different states of health and to ask the right sample. As Menzel puts it: 'we see how important it is to ask people explicitly QALY bargain questions and to consult a major percentage of people with experience of serious impairments'.[33] If this is done Menzel is quite happy to regard the consent of a small sample of the population obtained via a questionnaire as binding on society as a whole. 'With a good enough initial sample of others', he writes, 'it's acceptable to presume our consent to the trade-offs they chose.'[34]

This is truly staggering. We would effectively be committed to sacrificing our own lives in some circumstances on the results of a questionnaire based on a small sample population. And, to add insult to injury, we would be told we had consented to be sacrificed! Menzel previously noted that 'presumed consent arguments carry moral weight only when there is some good reason for not having obtained people's actual consent to the bargain question'.[35] Having noted that this may seem to rob QALYs of the moral force of consent he says blithely, 'To most of us this is not bothersome' and the reason is simply 'it would not be possible to approach everyone who might be affected . . . in the detail which would give us any confidence in the meaningfulness of the results'.[36]

Even politicians have never gone this far! Though the same reasoning might make attractive to them the prospect of abolishing general elections in favour of selecting governments by small sampling along the lines of opinion polls. However, arguably selecting a government is much less dangerous or consequential than decisions about QALYs. So, having started out by suggesting that whatever moral force QALYs

[32] Ibid. 8.
[33] Ibid. 14.
[34] Ibid. 13.
[35] Ibid. 9.
[36] Ibid. 13.

have rests on the fact that they are the people's choice, Menzel has in fact abandoned the idea of consent altogether. If no government has ever had the bare-faced cheek to claim a mandate on the basis of a questionnaire put to a small sample of the population (in the case of QALYs actually seventy or so subjects!) we can assume that it is not plausible as an indicator of consent.

But if there is no actual nor implied consent for the introduction of QALYs, might there be some other model which would indicate that we must accept them?

Hypothetical Consent

One obvious candidate is that provided by John Rawls in his *A Theory of Justice*.[37] If the QALY bargain is a good bargain wouldn't it be chosen by people in the original position? That is by people met together to choose the principles which will govern the society into which they will emerge but temporarily ignorant of all personal knowledge which would be of use to them in advantaging themselves in the arrangements that are to be made. Wouldn't such people be willing to trade off a large chance of a possibly small benefit—most will grow old—against a small chance of a large benefit, and so build the QALY bargain into their contract. And if it would be chosen by such people, doesn't this hypothetical consent not only give us the consent we need, but also show that QALYs are not only just but also impartial. For if they would be chosen by people ignorant of whether or not they would actually gain or lose by their choice and ignorant indeed of the identities of any of the people who would gain or lose, but simply because they were the best bargain for which they could opt, then such people would choose impartially. And doesn't this show that QALYs are not after all discriminatory?

The first point to notice is that, as Dworkin has powerfully shown, hypothetical contracts do not provide an independent argument for the fairness of enforcing their terms:

> Suppose you and I are playing poker and we find, in the middle of a hand, that the deck is one card short. You suggest that we throw the hand in, but I refuse because I know I am going to win and I want the money in the pot. You might say that I would certainly have agreed to that procedure had the possibility of the deck being short been raised in advance. But your point is not that I am somehow committed to throwing the hand in by an agreement I never made. Rather you use the device of a hypothetical agreement to make a point that

[37] John Rawls, *A Theory of Justice* (Cambridge, Mass.: Harvard University Press, 1972).

might have been made without that device, which is that the solution recommended is so obviously fair and sensible that only someone with an immediate contrary interest could disagree. Your main argument is that your solution is fair and sensible, and the fact that I would have chosen it myself adds nothing of substance to that argument. If I am able to meet the main argument nothing remains, rising out of your claim that I would have agreed, to be answered or excused.[38]

In Rawlsian scholarship there is much argument about just what people in the original position would choose. But as many critics of Rawls have pointed out, the mere presence of a veil of ignorance behind which people are required to make decisions, does not ensure that the decisions that are made will be just or indeed impartial. People in the original position might choose a slave-owning society, gambling on emerging as a master rather than as a slave. But the mere fact that they did not know at the time of deciding which they would be, does not make slavery just nor guarantee that slaves are not the victims of discrimination. If we suppose that say a small number of wretched slaves would support a large community living in the lap of luxury, then it might well be in anyone's interests to take the bargain—this might give them their best chance of benefiting from the contract. Indeed the two principles that Rawls believes emerge from the original position are plausible as the two principles of justice, not because they emerge from the original position but again, as Dworkin has argued, because they will strike us as fair and sensible.

So, the mere fact (if it is a fact) that QALYs would or might plausibly be chosen in the original position does not guarantee their claim to impartiality, nor does it establish them as just or fair. The veil of ignorance essential to the original position deprives the contractors of the ability to advantage themselves in any arrangements they choose and thus gives them a strong motive to choose arrangements that will benefit them most whatever position they turn out to occupy in the society into which they will emerge. This is one explanation of the choice of the two very abstract principles that Rawls believes would be chosen. However, the proviso of choosing under conditions of ignorance cannot guarantee that the arrangements chosen will operate impartially.

Indeed Dworkin argues, I believe conclusively, that the plausibility of Rawls' theory of justice arises from the fact that it presupposes a deep moral theory which Dworkin identifies as a highly abstract theory of equality.[39] It is, so Dworkin argues, this theory that explains the choice

[38] Ronald Dworkin, op. cit., 151.
[39] Ibid.

of the two principles and which gives them their plausibility. They are consistent it is true with having been chosen in the original position—but then so are many others. Their force arises not from this but from the fact that they are expressions of the deep moral theory which embodies a conception of equality of concern and respect. And this right to equality of concern and respect is, as Dworkin argues, 'one right, therefore, that does not emerge from the contract, but is assumed as the fundamental right must be, in its design'.[40]

It is the assumption of this principle in the design of the original position that makes that position plausible as a device for testing ideas about justice and which helps to explain why the two principles that Rawls believes to be generated by this device strike us as plausible if they do. These two principles it will be remembered are that each person must have the largest share of political liberty that is compatible with a like liberty for all and that inequalities in things like wealth and material resources, political power and other substantial advantages are justifiable only in so far as they operate to the absolute advantage of the worst off members of society.

Now QALYs of course are about as inimical to this second principle as it is possible to be. For so far from operating to the absolute benefit of the worst off members of society they operate to their absolute detriment. For arguably the worst off members of society are those with the poorest quality of life coupled with the shortest life expectancy.

The plausibility of the original position as a device for testing ideas of justice would be discredited if it was shown that it led to the reverse of this second principle and to violating the equality principle. So that neither Rawls' original position nor ideas about hypothetical consent lend any plausibility to QALYs nor do they add anything to their claims to be impartial.

We have almost reached a conclusion but before leaving these issues to the mature judgment of the reader I must take up a couple of the points that have been made by Michael Lockwood in his stimulating discussion of these issues.[41]

VI. Lockwood's Objections

Ageism Again

In his postscriptorial update to 'Quality of Life and Resource Allocation', Lockwood makes two points about the fairness or otherwise of using age or life expectancy as a justification for preference in the allocation of medical resources. The first suggests that I am:

[40] Ibid.
[41] See this volume, pp. 33–55.

. . . mistaken in thinking that the QALY approach is ageist. For it is not true that QALY maximization involves discriminating against older patients as such; what it discriminates against is those with relatively low life expectancy [after treatment].

Now of course I am not mistaken in thinking this because I don't think it. I made this very clear in my earlier 'QALYfying the Value of Life' and indeed earlier in this paper.[42] What I did in fact argue above is still true, namely, that 'wherever treatment postpones death . . . it will, other things being equal, be the case that younger people have more life expectancy to gain from treatment than do older people'.

But Lockwood believes that there is nothing wrong with discriminating against the old. Indeed he suggests that what's wrong with QALYs is that they fail 'to be ageist when they should be rather than being ageist when they should not be'.[43] So there are two points that can bear further consideration: They are:

(1) Are QALYs ageist or are they not,
and
(2) Ought they to be ageist and indeed should any method of resource allocation deliberately discriminate against the old?

Lockwood believes QALYs are not ageist, that is they do not unjustly discriminate against the old because:

The situation is parallel to that of selecting amongst applicants for a job that calls for a high degree of physical strength. In such circumstances, men would be likely to be chosen in preference to women; but that would not be sexist, provided that weaker men were not chosen in preference to demonstrably stronger women.[44]

Lockwood has two thoughts here. The first is that because QALYs do not discriminate against the old *as such* they are not discriminatory. I have dealt with this point above (pp. 84 and 85) arguing that measures can be *de facto* discriminatory however well intentioned their design. However, Lockwood's second thought, which relies on a parallel with applicants for a job seems even less happy. The idea that particular jobs require particular *qualifications* and that those inadequately qualified may be rejected need not raise questions of justice at all. All that is required is that an individual's qualifications are not disregarded out of prejudice and that the question of what counts as a qualification be not arbitrarily or prejudicially decided so as to exclude certain people who

---

[42] Harris, 'QALYfying the Value of Life', p. 119, and in this paper, pp. 79–80, *supra*.

[43] Lockwood, *supra* p. 54.

[44] *Supra* p. 53.

might none the less do an adequate job. (Does police work require that candidates be five foot ten inches in height?—Do particular societies benefit from the presence of black police officers more than they benefit from recruiting exclusively from those with the highest grades in examinations?[45]) If these criteria are met I'm far from sure that Lockwood's example is clearly free from the possibility of sexism in employment but we need not pursue that point now.

But, we are not talking about selecting applicants for jobs, we are talking about selecting who will live and who will die. The point of the equality principle is in large part to remind us that people do not have to *qualify* for the right to society's protection against measures that constitute attacks upon their very life. The idea that one might have to provide appropriate qualifications before being permitted to continue to exist cannot be sensibly compared with the idea of qualifying for a job. People are treated equally with respect to competition for a job if appropriate qualifications are given equal weight. But people are not treated equally as persons if some are thought more worthy of survival than others. The proper parallel with employment would be if some people were ruled out as candidates for any employment at all. Now this does very often happen with the old, and with those of retirement age— which brings us to Lockwood's more substantial claim, which is that discrimination against the old is justifiable, not that it isn't after all discrimination.

The Fair Innings Argument

Lockwood's further claim is that discrimination against the old ought to be built into any system of resource allocation precisely because so far from being unjust it is perfectly fair to discriminate against the old. Lockwood's reasons for accepting this are, he says, that he is impressed 'as Harris is not by what is commonly referred to as "the fair innings argument"'.[46] The articulation of this argument and the problems which attend it are complex and I cannot hope to do them justice here. However some things can be said. The first is that it is simply not true that I am not impressed by this argument. I outlined the structure of this argument, I believe sympathetically, and indeed called it 'the fair innings argument' some time ago.[47] And I made clear then, and still believe, that it contains a strong expression of what we intuitively feel about the justice of hard choices between lives. However it does have its problems which are not inconsiderable. I am happy with Lockwood's

[45] See Ronald Dworkin op. cit. Ch. 9.
[46] Lockwood, *supra* p. 50.
[47] See my *The Value of Life,* 91ff.

formulation of the essence of this argument which is:

> . . . an older person seeking dialysis, for example, has already by
> definition lived for longer than a younger person. To treat the older
> person, letting the younger person die, would thus be inherently
> inequitable in terms of years of life lived: the younger person would
> get no more years than the relatively few he had already had, whereas
> the older person, who has already had more than the younger person,
> will get several years more.[48]

I accept that thus formulated the fair innings argument outlines a
principle of selection which has some claim to be called a fair principle.
I also agree with Lockwood that QALYs are not an expression of this
principle. I am not, however, ultimately attracted to such a principle
and I believe, for the same reasons, that while it has some claims to
fairness it has also features which involve profound injustice and that
these are stronger.

Again, I can only rehearse them briefly here.[49] The first point to
make is that the 'fair innings argument' requires that we always give
preference to younger people in the allocation of life saving or death
postponing resources. Wherever there is an emergency we should save
'youngest first'. If one imagines a lecture hall filled with undergradu-
ates, it is not unequivocally clear that those in their first year should be
saved at the expense of those in the third if the hall catches fire. It is not
obvious that third year students ought to accept such an arrangement as
fair or that they should regard it as morally binding upon themselves.
Many would think it invidious to select on any but a random basis in
such circumstances. The fair innings argument as presented by Lockwood involves locating the injustice of premature death exclusively (or
at any rate principally) in the amount of potential life-time that the
individual thereby loses relative to others. But there is an important
sense in which all those who face premature death face the same loss—
the same tragedy. Each stands to lose everything—life itself. It is unjust
automatically to visit this loss, this tragedy, upon those who happen to
be a few years or a few minutes older than rivals.

To bring out this point with any adequacy I would need, as I do
elsewhere,[50] to defend a view of just what it is that makes life valuable. I
believe that the value of life can only sensibly be taken to be that value
that those alive place upon their lives. Consequently if you and I are of
different ages but we both want to live, then it is unfair to prefer your
life to mine simply because you are three months younger.

[48] Lockwood, *supra,* p. 50.
[49] Harris, op. cit. Ch. 5.
[50] Ibid. Ch. 1, 2.

John Harris

Lockwood argues rightly that '[f]airness must be assessed on the basis of someone's life as a whole'.[51] But taking your life and mine as a whole involves the judgment that when either of us dies prematurely (that is when our existence could be prolonged) we are each deprived of the same thing, namely the chance to live a whole life and are thus equally adversely affected irrespective of the fact that you have lived a few months less of a whole life than have I.

The case in which the idea of a whole life becomes more meaningful is that in which 'whole life' is stipulated to be a given term, say three score years and ten in which an individual is deemed to have or had have the chance of living a whole life. Premature death would then be death before the expiry of the term. In this case when choosing between the lives of those who have lived a full term and those who have not, it would be unfair to prefer the lives of those who have already lived a full term. However, this is not the conception of fair innings that is used by Lockwood nor is it employed in the theory of QALYs, so both its interest and the problems of using it may be left for discussion elsewhere.[52]

In any event the issue between Lockwood and me here must be resolved if at all by deciding which of us paints the more attractive picture of a principle of equality. One which claims that persons are valued equally when each person's wish to go on living is given equal weight, that is when the value that each person places upon their own existence is given equal weight. Or, one in which peoples lives are valued relative to the amount of life-time they have managed to accumulate—the value diminishing *pro rata* relative to others according to how long their life has already lasted. I cannot say more about this particular issue here.[53]

Nevertheless, we both agree I think, that however this issue is resolved it goes no way to making QALYs more attractive. However, there is one more issue between us that can be more quickly resolved. It concerns what I have called 'economism'.

Economism Re-visited

Lockwood now accepts my point that giving priority to conditions which are cheap to treat is unfair to those who just happen to have conditions which are expensive to treat. He now however suggests that failing to treat as many people as we can would be more unfair still. I agree in part. By that I mean that I think we have two equally plausible

[51] Lockwood, *supra* p. 50.
[52] See my *The Value of Life* for a fuller account.
[53] See ibid.

94

moral principles at work here and that they pull in opposite directions. When this is true some means of doing justice to each must be found and it is not enough merely to opt for one.

The powerful argument that I accept is that equality requires that each person must be given equal weight and it follows that more count for more. So favouring cheap treatments means that we can treat more and this accords with our principle. However, my criticism of QALYs is that they automatically direct us to channel funds to conditions that are cheap to treat and this can lead to systematic disadvantage to the poor (those who cannot afford the treatment their illness requires) and that this too is unjust.

Equality requires both that we treat as many people as we can and that we ensure so far as is possible that certain sorts of people be not systematically ignored. Other things being equal we should always rescue as many people as we can. But other things are not always equal. For example, others things being equal it will always be more expensive to treat people who live further from medical centres than those who live nearby. A QALY style expedient would simply involve ignoring the plight of outlying citizens. But a society which makes any claim to treating all its citizens as equals must make some provision for those who live in more remote parts of the country. And it must do this even at some increased cost. If it fails to do so it violates the equality principle.

The same is true of many other areas of social provision. The handicapped may cost more to educate or to house but a society which used *that* as a reason for ignoring their special needs would not be one which accorded them equality of concern and respect and most would not think much of its claim to be a fair society either.

Now maybe our society, any society, ought (sometimes?) to violate this principle. Often more will simply count for more. But where this leads to systematic disadvantage to particular groups—the poor, the old, the handicapped and so on and particularly where such groups are also vulnerable or weak for other reasons it will be unjust simply and always to go to the aid of the more fortunate majority.

VI. Conclusion

I have concentrated in this paper not so much in showing in detail the consequences of accepting QALYs as a measure either of efficiency in health care or as a method of establishing priorities. Rather I have sought to demonstrate that QALYs violate the equality principle on any plausible interpretation of that principle and cannot sustain their claim to be impartial or acceptable because they are what people either do, or would, or might hypothetically, want. The point of the equality principle is to set moral limits to the legitimate exercise of people's wants, when the exercise of those wants may unfairly, adversely affect others.

I have talked at times as if the equality principle was only one principle. Of course there are a number of principles that lay claim to being principles of equality. For the purposes of this paper however it has not been necessary to either distinguish or to adjudicate between them since QALYs violate, as I have argued, any plausible version of the equality principle.

How Much is Due to Health Care Providers?

ALBERT WEALE

How much by way of economic reward is due to health care providers?

Although this problem usually presents itself as a practical matter of policy, it has buried within it a number of philosophical issues, for it can be regarded as a question in the theory of economic justice. The formal principle of justice is that we should render persons what is due to them. But on what consideration in the case of health care providers can we make an assessment of what is due?

The answer we give to this question has significant implications for the ethical appraisal of the allocation of resources in the health care system. Some of the most difficult issues of ethical appraisal emerge when we consider the problems of allocating potentially life-saving resources between different groups of patients. Many of the most significant current issues in medical ethics—the role of QALYs, the meaning of equality and the economic evaluation of life—find their point of reference in the 'tragic choices'[1] that are created when there are insufficient resources to meet apparently legitimate medical need. Yet, as Robert Evans[2] has pointed out, it is a simple matter of accounting identity that health care expenditures must equal health providers' incomes. So, in asking how we limit or allocate costly health care resources, we are implicitly offering an answer to the question of how much we should pay providers. I hope by seeking an answer explicitly to that question to throw light on the problems that are raised when considering ethically the allocation of health care resources.

There may be advantages in considering the problems of allocation from the point of view of provider incomes. Proposals for cost containment in health care often have the effect of limiting access to resources by increasing the burdens upon consumers. This effect is obvious in the UK's National Health Service (NHS) where queues for various operations, for example hip replacements, or non-referral by primary care

[1] G. Calabresi and P. Bobbitt, *Tragic Choices* (New York: Norton, 1978).
[2] Robert G. Evans, 'The Spurious Dilemma: Reconciling Medical Progress and Cost Control', *Quarterly Journal of Health Service Management* **4** No. 1 (1986), 25–34.

physicians, as for example with renal dialysis[3], place significant burdens on particular groups of patients and their relatives. Such effects are also apparent in health insurance schemes as found in the United States. To increase co-payments, co-insurance and deductibles as devices for cutting down on health care demand means that patients have to bear burdens of increased pain and suffering as well as increased economic cost. It is also difficult to believe that the twenty million Americans or so who have no health insurance cover (see President's Commission, p. 93)[4] are not also not bearing the consequence of a policy to reduce the rise in health care costs. Although no responsible approach to the ethics of health care resources can avoid the possibility that there may be a duty on citizens to suffer and die cheaply, neither can it avoid asking whether there is not a duty on providers to care and cure cheaply.

The examples of both Canada and the United Kingdom suggest that control of providers' incomes may be a crucial means for controlling cost escalation. The relatively low proportion of national income that is devoted to health care in the UK in part reflects low wages and salaries throughout much of the hospital care sector. In Canada sole-source funding, by means of the monopoly of federally funded insurance programmes, has not only maintained a limit on the growth of health care expenditure since its introduction, but it has done so by means of controlling physician incomes, leaving a high level of public satisfaction with the quantity and quality of care.[5] Clearly, however, such a process cannot continue indefinitely. To control the growth of physician incomes runs the risk of lowering their incomes relative to other groups. The prospect of large-scale emigration means that governments have to be prudent in running this risk for fear of losing expensively trained personnel; a concern with economic justice ought to make policy-makers sensitive to the limits to which they can reduce incomes.

Providers are a heterogeneous group. As well as those directly involved in the provision of health care, they include builders, equipment suppliers and drug companies, in addition to the administrative and ancillary staff who support the direct providers. However it is direct providers—doctors, dentists, nurses and other specified health

[3] S. Challah, A. J. Wing, R. Bower, B. Morris and S. Schroeder, 'Negative Selection of Patients for Dialysis and Transplantation in the United Kingdom', *British Medical Journal* **288** (1984), 1119–1122.

[4] President's Commission for the Study of Ethical Problems in Medicine and Biomedical and Behavioural Research, *Securing Access to Health Care: Ethical Implications of Differences in the Accessibility of Health Services* (Washington, DC: Government Printing Office, 1983).

[5] Robert G. Evans, 'Health Care in Canada: Patterns of Funding and Regulation', in G. McLachlan and A. Maynard (eds), *The Private/Public Mix for Health* (London: Nuffield Provincial Hospitals Trust, 1982), 369–424.

personnel—who are the focus for this paper. This is not merely a matter of convenience when one is having to draw the line somewhere. In all health care systems wages and salaries are a high proportion of health expenditures: for example, the English health authorities in 1984–85 spent over seventy per cent of their incomes on NHS staff salaries.[6] Moreover, I shall argue that special considerations apply to direct providers which makes the valuation of their services particularly difficult.

I shall also limit my treatment in one other significant way. A proper treatment of fair rewards in medicine ought to develop principles that suggest relativities among subgroups of direct providers. This task is desirable not least because technological changes in medicine create a new division of labour between different members of those involved in care. For example, nurses and clerical officers have routine responsibility for the care of renal dialysis patients. Moreover, *changes* in relativities will feed through to the estimates of QALYs for different clinical conditions; if primary care physicians are paid more relative to other health personnel, then the cost per QALY of those conditions treated by primary care physicians rises accordingly. So, to the extent to which we are worried by implicit discrimination in the QALY approach, we ought to think about the fairness of the salary relativities that are involved. However, although an obviously important matter, I must plead shortage of space, and competence, to treat such issues in this paper.

Problems of Method

It is sometimes argued that the appraisal of the salaries for particular groups of workers is not something that can be brought within the scope of a theory of justice. Brittan (p. 123)[7] for example argues that there are too many plausible candidates for consideration as a just basis of allocation to yield a consistent outlook. Desert, scarcity, comparability, equality and so on will yield contradictory prescriptions, so that no complete and consistent ordering of existing claims is possible. Although he does not argue the point in detail, Rawls's restriction of the principles of justice to the 'basic structure' has the same effect. There are arguments therefore both of practicality and of philosophical theory suggesting that it is not possible to discuss the fairness of income returns to providers.

[6] DHSS, *The Health Service in England, Annual Report 1985–86* (London: HMSO, 1986).

[7] Samuel Brittan, 'The Economic Contradictions of Democracy', in A. King (ed.), *Why is Britain Becoming Harder to Govern?* (London: BBC, 1976).

The consequence of this approach is to relegate considerations of fairness from the appraisal of provider incomes. Incomes would then be decided purely on grounds of economic efficiency by the test of opportunity cost, that is the willingness of citizens to forgo other desirable goods and services for the sake of their health, and provider incomes would simply measure the opportunity cost to the economy of employing people in the health sector rather than in some other line of business. On this account any further test of provider incomes is merely otiose.

One problem with this approach is that it is inconsistent with the principles upon which health care financing is organized in all economically advanced liberal democracies. Provider incomes will yield a reasonable measure of opportunity cost under one of two conditions: either markets are functioning perfectly so that consumer willingness to pay registers opportunity cost; or public institutions are amalgamating individual preferences in such a way as to yield a measure of perceived costs. Neither of these conditions are satisfied in the case of health care provision. For various reasons the health care market is riddled with imperfections which create a divergence between perceived and actual cost. Public institutions are beset by the Arrow problem: there simply is no reasonable way to amalgamate individual preferences into a social choice. It is simply implausible to believe that efficiency is attained merely by ignoring anything but the basic structure of economic organization.

Even if efficiency were attainable, however, there are reasons for modifying the operation of any mechanism that was designed merely to minimize the total cost of producing a specified volume of goods and services in the economy. Willingness to pay is complemented by willingness to provide. But some suppliers of labour may be prepared to supply more to the health care sectors of the economy for a given return than they would supply to other sectors because they have a belief in the intrinsically worthwhile nature of medicine. Thus nursing recruitment in the United Kingdom has traditionally operated on a high recruitment, low wage, higher turnover principle by trading on the disposition to be of service.[8] To suppose that there are no issues of fairness that are raised by such examples is merely to beg the question as to whether providers of labour can be exploited by virtue of the motivation they bring to their work.

There is one further reason why we cannot restrict considerations of fairness merely to the basic structure but we have to consider the fairness of health provider incomes as an issue in its own right. Within

[8] Michael O'Higgins, *Health Spending—A Way to Sustainable Growth* (London: Institution of Health Service Management, 1987).

the policy-making institutions of the UK provider incomes are thought to be a matter of fairness. The Review Body of Doctors' and Dentists' Remuneration defined its task in a recent report as follows: 'to consider all the factors we believe to be relevant and on that basis to judge what levels of remuneration are necessary to reward fairly the contribution that doctors and dentists make to the NHS' (p. 2).[9] When confronted by an existing and well-respected institutional practice, the correct philosophical response is to seek to offer a rational appraisal of the principles on which it might operate, not act in the hope that by ignoring it the issues will go away.

A Proposal

The proposal that I wish to advance is that provider incomes should be no less than those providers would have received had they entered their next most preferred occupation instead of going into the health sector. The test of what is due to providers is thus one which protects them against a downward pressure on incomes in so far as that applies to medical personnel in particular, but not against a downward pressure in so far as that applies to high earners in general. I shall refer to this as the principle of comparability.

Two points need to be made by way of clarifying this principle. The first is that the proper measure of income ought to be expected lifetime income and not simply any presumptively relevant comparison at a given point in time or career. For different people earnings are variously distributed across their lifetimes, and what matters for the point of principle is what an annual income sums to over the course of a person's life discounting for the burden of deferred consumption and the need to take uncertainty into consideration. Moreover, the costs of training, including forgone earnings during the period of training, ought to be deducted from the sum in question. Such adjustments are not minor in effect. US data suggest that when allowance is made for the cost of training, physician incomes drop from a ratio of five to one relative to average worker incomes to a ratio of two to one (Menzel, p. 218).[10] I have not seen comparable estimates for the United Kingdom, but the point of principle stands just the same. It is not sufficient to observe that virtually all consultants are in the upper half of the top one per cent of the earnings distributions, as they are (Review

[9] Review Body on Doctors' and Dentists' Remuneration, *Sixteenth Report, 1986* Cmnd. 9788 (London: HMSO, 1986).

[10] Paul Menzel (1983), *Medical Costs, Moral Choices* (New Haven, Conn.: Yale University Press, 1983).

Body, p. 47);[11] it is also necessary to take into account time spent in training and time spent as junior doctors at the beginning of their career only halfway up the earnings distribution.

The second point is that the principle of comparability is intended to act as a statistical norm and not as a counterfactual comparison. To say that providers should earn no less than they could have earned in their next most preferred occupation is not to make a statement about what a particular group of individuals could have earned had they chosen different occupations. We can, however, make statistical comparisons between different types of people. We can say for example what the earnings expectation is of workers with particular qualifications and career opportunities. It is such statistical comparisons that are relevant to the principle being advanced. In other words the principle is that health care providers should not earn less over their lifetime than persons with similar qualifications from the same generation.

The effect of this second aspect of the proposal is to make the operation of the principle less generous than some providers would like. It is a common ploy among those who favour high physician incomes to pick on some particular occupation (airline pilots are a favourite) and to argue that incomes for physicians should match those of that occupational group (see material in Daniels, p. 130).[12] By averaging over the expected income streams of a broadly designated reference group, the present proposal avoids the evident lack of good faith that such arguments rest upon.

The proposal is asymmetric in its implications. It does not say that provider incomes are just if they are above the level of the hypothetical reference group. It merely says that it would be unjust to allow them to fall below it. As it stands the principle is agnostic on the point of whether provider incomes ought to be above the reference level, allowing either that they should, or that those who finance health services are entitled to keep earnings at that reference level, or that it is a matter of moral indifference what happens above that level. On the other hand the proposal does carry the clear implication that a cost containment programme would be using unjust means if it sought to achieve its objectives by driving provider incomes below that level.

Despite its modest scope, the principle does clash with the most sophisticated alternative proposal, namely that providers should receive equal net benefits from their occupational choice compared to others (Menzel, pp. 224–229).[13] Why prefer the less radical proposal of comparability to the more radical principle of equality? Since the issue

---

[11] Ibid.
[12] Norman Daniels, *Just Health Care* (Cambridge University Press, 1985).
[13] Ibid.

is usually discussed in terms of physician income (rather than, say, nurses) where the expectation is that application of the equality principle would indicate a substantial reduction, I shall discuss the issue with respect to that case.

Cost control programmes bear upon three aspects of the health care system: the incomes of providers; the costs borne by patients; and the costs borne by the ultimate financers, be they citizen taxpayers or health insurance customers. Greater cost containment would be achieved if physician incomes were reduced to accord with the net equality principle, but the effect of this approach is to place a disproportionate share of the burden on physicians and not on the other groups who are involved in the problem. One reason why this is so is that career opportunities once passed over are often not recoverable. The skills acquired through training and the on-the-job expertise that comes with experience lock people into certain career patterns from which they cannot effectively escape. To pursue a policy of reducing physician incomes without at the same time reducing other comparable incomes would therefore be to exploit the situation of those who, once they have embarked upon a career, only have limited choices available to them. Of course if there were a general policy of reducing high earnings so as to accord with the net equality principle, then the principle of comparability would allow physician incomes to fall in line with the secular trend. In this instance the net equality principle is a special case of the comparability principle, and high earners would be disproportionately bearing the costs of health expenditure containment programmes.

It might be argued that the worry about exploiting the limited choices that people had once they had embarked on a career was merely a problem of transition. Suppose we could engineer a situation in which the rewards to physicians were no higher than the net average whilst members of other comparable groups were still earning more than the average. Problems of adequate incentives might prevent our reaching this point, but if we had engineered such a situation the incentive problem would, *ex hypothesi*, have been overcome. (The strength of applications to medical schools suggests that we could move substantially in that direction.) Provided we had secured sufficient recruitment, we should have solved our cost containment problem and those recruited would presumably have consented to forgo the extra income they could have earned in other occupations. Is there any reason for saying that the principle of comparability should apply in such a situation?

To claim that comparability ought to apply is to deny that consent to a wage-level always makes that wage just. Clearly consent will sometimes be sufficient to render just a particular wage-level, but only provided that the level in question falls within specific limits. The question to be raised in the present case is whether or not those limits have been exceeded. People enter careers for many motives. However, one reason that is often prominent in medicine is the altruistic desire to be of service to others. In so far as this motive does obtain, it would not be surprising if health planners could successfully attract recruits to medicine whilst simultaneously lowering relative salaries. However, to pursue this aim as a conscious element of public policy would be manipulative and exploitive. If people consent to a wage-level, that level may still be unjust if the only condition under which it can be so low is that its acceptance requires a strong moral commitment to the career in question.

The notion of exploitation that is doing the work here can be stated as follows: it is wrong to obtain a service from other persons at cost to themselves merely because you are able to take advantage of their altruistic motivations. The cost that is being borne by providers under a policy of driving their incomes below the level of comparability is the loss of what they would have earned had they entered a different occupation to which they could have gained entry. There is of course a sense in which they have freely chosen this course of action: the moving principle was in themselves. But there is another sense in which such a choice is not free. People cannot distance themselves from their motivation and character. To trade an altruistic motivation therefore is to take advantage of a facet of someone's life over which, in a sense, they have little control.

The above represents an argument for upholding the principle of comparability. However, it may be objected that the principle of comparability is vulnerable from another point of view. Although the principle of comparability requires that economic returns do not drop below a certain level, it does not require that they rise above that level. Yet it may be argued that this is unjust. Just as we think it appropriate to avoid exploitation by refusing to trade on others' altruistic motives, so we might think it appropriate to recognize that those same motivations create a claim of merit or desert entitling persons to a reward. Is it therefore possible to supplement the comparability principle by an appeal to the principle of desert which would indicate a higher level of physician incomes?

It is useful when considering claims of merit or desert to distinguish between two senses of the notion: moral desert and institutional desert (Weale, pp. 158–168).[14] The distinction between the two notions rests upon the type of characteristics that are thought to form the ground or

[14] Albert Weale, *Political Theory and Social Policy* (London: Macmillan, 1983).

basis of the claim of desert. Moral desert is based on personal qualities that have a general moral relevance, for example exceptional courage or fortitude. Institutional desert by contrast is based on personal qualities that are specific to some social practice or occupation, for example being particularly well qualified in some skill. Naturally this is not a hard and fast distinction, if only because some personal qualities, for example honesty, are not only of general moral significance, but also have value for a wide range of specific social and economic activities. None the less, the distinction is an important one because it explains why some skills that have no significance outside of the economic or social activity within which they occur, for example the manual dexterity that is part of being a good surgeon, might merit reward. Lack of manual dexterity connotes no moral failing; its presence therefore cannot form a basis for moral merit. However, it may form the basis for institutional desert if the institution in question needs to foster the development of such skills.

Altruistic motivation by itself cannot form the basis for desert claims. Desert rewards attainment rather than motivation; and even when it rewards effort it can logically do so only if the effort stands proxy for an attained and realizable capacity (Weale, pp. 161–162).[15] So the general moral qualities that might dispose persons to take up a medical career cannot of themselves form a claim of merit for higher than otherwise expected rewards. The specific skills that the institution of medicine needs to encourage may of course form the basis for claims of institutional desert, and some of these skills, for example a commitment to relieve suffering or a willingness to see things from the patients' point of view, may have general relevance. But the purpose of granting institutional desert claims is to foster the purpose that the institution is there to achieve.

If claims of desert in this context have an institutional character, so that they function to promote the institution and practice of medicine, then a number of conclusions follow about the way in which desert may serve as an argument for economic reward. The principal conclusion is that desert will function as a principle for varying economic reward within the medical profession, but not between the medical profession and other groups of workers. That is to say, desert will provide reasons for raising certain physicians above the average for other medical personnel because these particular individuals display the personal qualities that medicine needs to flourish. By contrast, desert will not provide a reason for raising average incomes above those of comparable groups.

[15] Ibid.

There is already in place in the UK system of health care planning a system of merit awards by which consultants thought to be deserving are granted increases above the basic scale rates of pay. (The value of these awards should not be underestimated: the highest award virtually doubles NHS derived pay.) There is much criticism about the manner in which these awards are made, not only in terms of the secrecy of the procedure but also in terms of the criteria that are employed. However, that criticism is not relevant to the theme of this paper. What is relevant is that if the argument about the basis of desert has force, then merit awards should not be used to raise the average physician's income. Since desert cannot be used as an argument for raising physician's pay above the average of comparable workers, the granting of merit awards ought to affect the dispersion of individual physician salaries around a given central value rather than increase that value.

Implications

The principle that physicians should not suffer economic loss as a result of their career choice is complex to put into practice. It requires an econometric estimate of the rates of the return to persons with a specified level of skill and qualifications over a given period of time. The practical device that is currently used by the Review Body is to compare physicians' income over time in terms of how well they are doing in the general earnings distribution. This bears a superficial resemblance to the comparability principle, and it may be the only practical solution currently available, but it should not be confused with the principle being advocated here. In effect the Review Body adopts the principle that physicians should receive an income comparable to what their occupational group has historically received, so that comparability on their interpretation implies that medical practitioners should not slip down the earnings distribution. The principle that is advocated here implies nothing about where groups of workers with particular skills should be in the earnings distribution. General changes in the economy, including changes in the provision of higher education and the developments of technology, may lead to medical practitioners and those who share their labour market skills either to fall or to rise in the earnings distribution. That is an empirical question; the principle of comparability does not imply that medical practitioners should occupy any particular place in the earnings distribution, although it does allow that the Review Body's practice may be a reasonable short-term ready-reckoner of where medical practitioners should be in the absence of more complete evidence.

One consequence of adopting the principle of comparability is that cost containment measures aimed at reducing physician earnings cannot be pursued in the absence of a more general incomes policy for high earners. In effect this is saying that if the burdens of cost containment policies are not to fall on patients or taxpayers and insurance payers, then those burdens cannot be assumed by the medical profession alone, but they must also be borne by high income recipients in the economy at large. However, the operation of the principle might well have an opposite effect on the economic returns of other health care workers. If those who are low paid within health services are granted the principle of comparability, then their incomes may well rise. In that case the issue would arise as to how to share the burdens of comparability.

A particular problem emerges when it is a matter of considering how the costs of maintaining physicians' incomes should be borne between patients and taxpayers. The implementation of the Review Body's proposals has often been arbitrary and unprincipled in this respect. The government has funded only part of the pay award recommended by the Review Body, arguing that the general economic situation prevents the funding of an award at the recommended level. The Review Body's response to this practice has been to say that it already seeks to take into account the general economic situation in making its recommendations, and that its independence and standing is threatened if its proposals are overridden in an arbitrary way. The consequence of this procedure is that the health authorities who have responsibility for administering the NHS have no choice but to pay the salary award, and find the unfunded increase from other sources, usually from reductions in the volume of services.

By such a process the cost of funding annual pay increases for doctors is divided between patients and taxpayers in an unprincipled way. The problem here is not that it is unreasonable to take into account the costs of providing health services to a given volume and quality. Clearly, it would be irrational to regard our health status as of infinite value, so that collectively or individually we should sacrifice all other desirable things. So there is no doubt that cost has to figure somewhere in the balance. The difficulty with the existing procedure for implementing pay awards is that the trade-offs involved are never made explicit, so that it is not clear what sacrifices in patient services is regarded by the government as making a proper contribution to the burden of health care costs. Lack of explicitness in decision-making threatens political accountability. If the implications of underfunding are not made clear, then the performance of a government in a representative democracy cannot be publicly ascertained. The issue of explicitness, therefore, makes clear the importance of implementation when considering principles of allocation.

Does the principle of comparability have an implication for the method by which physicians are paid as well as the size of their expected average return? Certainly there seems to be no direct link, but there may be an indirect one stemming from the principles of accountability implicit in a public system of health care. Different health care systems use a variety of methods of payment. The three most common systems are fee for service, capitation and direct salary. The NHS uses all three systems in different ways: health authority employees are salaried; general practitioners receive capitation payments for the number of patients on their list; and general practitioners are also reimbursed for specific services they render. Physicians in the private sector operate on a fee for service basis.

The ability to set incomes is dependent upon the type of payments system used. Clearly it is easiest to control the total remuneration by means of salaries. Capitation payments will control returns within limits, and fee for service will have varying effects depending on how it is structured. (All systems can have some perverse effects on the volume and quality of patient care: if you have ever wondered why your GP only allows you five minute appointments, ponder for a second the incentives implicit in the capitation system.) The type of payment system to be preferred will therefore depend upon how stringently one interprets the principle of comparability.

If one favours comparability as a target to be aimed at, then one would favour a salary structure; if one favours comparability as a lower limit below which physicians ought not to go, then one would be more tolerant of fee for service arrangements.

However, one's view on this matter is also likely to be influenced by much more fundamental beliefs about professional autonomy and the right of occupational groups to bargain over their terms and conditions of service. In particular, this concerns views about the proper process by which the burdens of health care costs are allocated to different groups. If one sees physicians as part of an autonomous profession, then payment systems which allow them to earn above the comparability minimum are appropriate; if one sees physicians are part of a wider public sphere of responsibility, then alternative payment systems are appropriate. None the less, whatever payment system is adopted, it is clear that cost escalation pressures are leading to greater accountability about practice.

It may be argued that theoretical speculation on these matters is otiose. The political power of doctors is such that they are able to negotiate payment arrangements that are to their advantage. Marmor[16] has shown in a cross-national study, for example, that doctors were able to negotiate a payment structure after public intervention that was

[16] T. R. Marmor, *Political Analysis and American Medical Care* (Cambridge University Press, 1983).

essentially the same as that prior to public intervention. When power is so manifest, what is a point of principle? Two answers may be given to this question. The first, and simpler of the two, is that there is a proper theoretical interest in description: we ought to be concerned if doctors can negotiate an arrangement that gives them more than they ought justly to claim, and, in order to be able to identify a situation in which this was the outcome, we need to be able to specify what is a just claim. The second answer is that the rhetoric of justice is part of the currency of power. When doctors bargain with governments about the structure of payments, they use the language of rights and duties as a device for establishing the legitimacy of their case. Governments too engage in similar rhetorical ploys. Hence, to analyse the point of principle is to understand something about the structure of power.

Philosophical analysis cannot, of course, issue in concrete prescription. But there ought to be a point somewhere between leaving the world exactly as it is and remoulding it entire closer to the heart's desire. If the practical problems of cost containment in health care are to be solved whilst respecting justice in the allocation of resources to patients, then some principled basis upon which providers are rewarded needs to be established. Whether the principle of comparability advanced in this paper could function as such a principle is, I hope, at least worth discussing.

Ethics and Efficiency in the Provision of Health Care

ALAN WILLIAMS

I. Introduction

1.1. A major purpose in nationalizing the provision of health care in the UK was to affect its distribution between people, and, in particular, to minimize the impact of willingness and ability to pay upon that distribution. It has never been clear, however, what alternative distribution rule is to apply. There is no shortage of rhetoric about 'equality' and 'need', but most of it is vacuous, by which I mean it does not lead to any clear operational guidelines about who should get priority and at whose expense. The closest we have got so far to such explicit guidelines has been the formulae which determine the *geographical* distribution of NHS funds, the driving force behind which is a notion of need based on relative mortality rates and on the demographic structure. The avowed objective is to bring about equal access for equal need irrespective of where in the UK you happen to be.[1]

1.2. Equal access for equal need says nothing about the efficiency of the services to which you have access, it being assumed that they will do you good, and that the more you have of them the more good they will do you. It also assumes that the range of services offered is the best that can be afforded. A further implication, seldom exposed to public discussion, is that unless a service can be provided equally across all geographical areas it should not be provided at all, for equal access for equal need is quite consistent with no access at all for some needs. Accessibility therefore seems a rather limited conceptual basis for a discussion of the distributive ethic.[2]

[1] For a fuller discussion of these issues see: N. Daniels, 'Equity of Access to Health Care: Some Conceptual and Ethical Issues', *Millbank Memorial Fund Quarterly* **60** (1982); P. A. West, 'Theoretical and Practical Equity in the NHS in England', *Social Science and Medicine;* **15** (1981), 118; C. Paton, 'The Policy of Resource Allocation and Its Ramifications: A Review', *Nuffield Provincial Hospitals Trust Occasional Paper, No 2* (1985); S. Birch and A. Maynard, 'The RAWP Review', *Centre for Health Economics, Discussion Paper 19* (University of York, 1986).

[2] A point made earlier by others, e.g. R. Steele, 'Marginal Met Need and

1.3. The difficulty about going beyond service *provision,* and examining instead service *benefits,* is that we have no *routine* data on the latter, and even research findings on the benefit of health care are patchy in both coverage and reliability. Just attempting to define, measure and value such benefits at individual level seems to excite people's passions, and what to me seems commonsense propositions (such as that people value *both* improvements in the quality of their lives *and* improvements in their life expectancy, and that therefore the health service should also attach positive values to both) engender vehement counter-propositions of a quite extreme kind (e.g. that increasing people's life expectancy must take absolute priority over improving people's quality of life).

1.4. I do not want to go over that well-trodden ground again here[3] but to concentrate instead on one specific ethical issue, which is: *is a particular improvement in health to be regarded as of equal value no matter who gets it; and, if not, what precisely is its relative value in accruing to one kind of person as opposed to another?*

1.5. Before plunging into that deep water, may I point out that in order to concentrate single-mindedly on the issue posed, the following circumscriptive propositions should be noted:

1.5.1. I assume that benefits have been defined, measured and valued in a manner that is acceptable to everybody. In order to be as neutral as possible on that matter, I will, for expositional simplicity, assume that the health benefit we are talking about is simply one additional year of healthy life expectancy, to be enjoyed between the same dates in calendar time by whoever gets it.

1.5.2. I also assume that the health care system is operating at such a high level of efficiency that it is not possible for it to offer anyone an extra year of healthy life expectancy without depriving someone else of that same prospect.

1.5.3. I further assume that the health care system has at its disposal exactly the right amount of resources, as agreed by the community generally.

Geographical Equity in Health Care', *Scottish Journal of Political Economy* **28** (1981); G. H. Mooney, 'Equity in Health Care: Confronting the Confusion', in *Effective Health Care* **I** (1983); G. de Jong, and F. F. H. Rutten, 'Justice and Health for All', *Social Science and Medicine* **17** (1983), 1091.

[3] See P. Kind, R. Rosser and A. Williams, 'Valuation of Quality of Life: Some Psychometric Evidence', in M. W. Jones-Lee (ed.), *The Value of Life and Safety* (North-Holland, 1982); A. Williams, 'Economics of Coronary Artery Bypass Grafting', **291** (1985), 326–329; J. Harris *Journal of Medical Ethics* (forthcoming, 1987).

1.5.4. In determining the appropriate answer to my question, we are trying to operate from behind the 'veil of ignorance' about our own possible future dependence on the health care system, i.e. we are trying to decide what is 'right' in a 'good' society, not what is most likely to be in our own personal interest.

1.5.5. Although the desired distribution rule is to be cast in terms of the distribution of *benefits*, it will in fact also *determine* the distribution of *access*, since the pattern of provision of health care (including its geographical pattern) will follow automatically from the distribution rule once that is linked to the production possibilities open to the health care system.

1.5.6. I am not necessarily seeking a *one-dimensional* distribution rule (any more than I seek a one-dimensional concept of benefit), but if there is more than one dimension that is to have weight, I shall need specific guidance about the 'trade-offs' between one dimension and another in all situations where they are both likely to apply.

1.5.7. Finally, my long-term intention is to conduct a survey of the population at large to find out what *they* think about these issues, and I am using this opportunity to explore one possible way in which these issues might be posed to ordinary citizens so that they could respond in an informed way to some carefully designed questions which are as unbiased as it is possible to make them.

1.6. I plan to tackle this task as follows:

Section II provides an example of the sort of thing I am trying to do, and examines the weaknesses of what I have done so far.

Section III lists and discusses briefly the implications of various possible dimensions of a distribution rule (e.g. need, non-discrimination, diminishing marginal value, dependent others, compensating discrimination, etc.).

Section IV outlines some possible approaches to the trade-off problem.

Section V reports where I have got to so far.

II. The Perceived Importance of Health at Different Life Stages

2.1. During 1985 a survey was conducted in York of 377 people randomly selected from the electoral register, who were interviewed about a variety of matters concerning health.[4] Amongst the many things

[4] For further details see Stephen J. Wright, 'Age, Sex and Health: A Summary of Findings from the York Health Evaluation Survey' *Discussion Paper 15* (Centre for Health Economics, University of York, May 1986). The full dataset from this survey has been lodged with the ESRC Survey Research Archive and is available there for secondary analysis by interested researchers.

we were interested in was whether people thought that health benefits were more valuable at some stages in people's lives than at other stages. So during the interview respondents were shown a list of ten life stages, and asked:

If a choice had to be made between them, in which of the following circumstances would you think it most important to keep people *in general* well?

Please chose the three sets of circumstances you judge to be most important.

After three had been chosen from the list, respondents were then asked

Now from these three sets of circumstances, which would you judge to be most important, and which next most important?

Their answers are set out in Table 1.

2.2. One of our interests was to test whether or not a consensus exists, and this was treated by looking at the relationship between the responses and the sociodemographic data we had collected from respondents. Given the intentional distribution of the ten life stages selected across the lifespan (from 'infancy' to 'getting very old'), age might be expected to be a major influence on choices. Thus older subjects could be expected to select later stages of life as the most important to which to ensure wellness out of a simple egocentrism or self-interest. Similarly sex might be expected to influence choices due to the relationships between the traditional sex roles and the life stages employed. Thus males might be expected to emphasize school and work-orientated phases of life ('starting school', 'starting work', 'at the peak of earning power', 'retirement') whilst females could be anticipated to emphasize life stages relevant to their role as carer and homemaker ('bringing up children', 'looking after elderly relatives'). Other sociodemographic variables with social role implications (e.g. marital status, work status) might also be expected to affect choices.

2.3. What emerged is that the two life stages 'when bringing up children' and 'as infants', which were by far the most often selected, also showed a high degree of consensus across both sexes and all age-groups. If one looks at each life stage separately to see whether there are significant differences in response by any background factor, it turned out that females placed relatively more weight on 'bringing up children' and 'caring for elderly relations' and males on 'setting up home for the first time' and 'when at peak of earning power', thereby reflecting traditional sex roles. Differences in response by other background factors were negligible.

2.4. That study was not a suitable vehicle for exploring the next phase of the enquiry, which is to find out *how much more weight* is to be given

Ethics and Efficiency in the Provision of Health Care

Table I. York health evaluation survey

'If a choice had to be made between them, in which of the following circumstances would you think it most important to keep people *in general* well? Please choose the three sets of circumstances you judge to be most important'. After being shown the list and choosing three, respondents were asked 'Now from these three sets of circumstances, which would you judge to be most important, and which next most important?'

	Most important		Next most important		Third choice	
	N	%	N	%	N	%
As infants	103	27·3	36	9·5	25	6·6
When starting school	24	6·4	16	4·2	25	6·6
When starting work	14	3·7	37	9·8	42	11·1
When setting up home for the first time	10	2·7	21	5·6	17	4·5
When bringing up children	124	32·9	102	27·1	42	11·1
When the peak of their earning power	15	4·0	19	5·0	23	6·1
When looking after elderly relatives	19	5·0	44	11·7	38	10·1
When just having retired from work	16	4·2	36	9·5	63	16·7
When coping with the death of a husband or wife	23	6·1	31	8·2	45	11·9
When getting very old	27	7·2	33	8·8	53	14·1
(Unuseable responses)	(2)	(0·5)	(2)	(0·5)	(4)	(1·1)
Total	377	100·0	377	100·0	377	100·0

to the more important life stages compared with the less important. What I need to elicit is something like Table II, which is entirely hypothetical, and which purports to indicate, against an average index value of 1·0, how much *more* important the above average life stages are, and how much *less* important the below average ones are. One of the problems I shall address later is precisely how one might best elicit such information.

2.5. For the time being these data are presented merely to whet the appetite. In the present context they would imply that in order to give one extra year of healthy life expectancy to an infant (valued at 2·75) it would be worth sacrificing about 10·5 years of healthy life expectancy

115

Table II. *Hypothetical data on the relative values of good health at different life stages*

As infants	2·75
When starting school	0·64
When starting work	0·37
When starting up home for the first time	0·26
When bringing up children	3·31
When at peak of earning power	0·40
When looking after elderly relatives	0·51
When just having returned from work	0·43
When coping with the death of spouse	0·61
When getting very old	0·72

1·00 = Standard value if no differentiation between life stages.

(each valued at 0·26) which might have been given to someone setting up home for the first time. It is at this level of specificity that the ethical problem of setting up distributional rules needs to be solved if it is going to yield clear operational guidance to those responsible for running the health care system.

III. Possible Distribution Rules

3.1. In section II the possibility was explored that 'life stages' might be a relevant dimension in a distribution rule for health benefits, and it did indeed elicit a very clear consensus that health benefits at some life stages are regarded as more valuable than at others. But 'life stages' are an amalgam of age-related elements and role-related elements (and possibly even implicit sex-role factors) so maybe it would be better to attempt a finer discrimination by separating out these different characteristics and dealing with them individually (at first, anyway, even though they may need to be combined later).

3.2. What I propose to do next, therefore, is to list, and examine briefly, some possible axes along which discrimination might be considered desirable on ethical grounds (i.e. features according to which someone might think that we *should* discriminate between people) and we can then consider the likely *consequences* of each such rule (i.e. who would benefit, and who would lose) compared with some 'standard' rule (with no implication that the 'standard' rule is ethically superior, though it might turn out to be).

3.3. The 'standard rule' I shall use is that a unit of health benefit (say 'an additional year of healthy life expectancy') is to be regarded as of equal value no matter who gets it. The data in Table I indicate that most people do not subscribe to this view, but that is of no consequence at present. In terms of Table II, this rule would mean that the numbers shown against each life stage would be 1·0 in each case. Thus in the distribution of health benefits the standard case would not discriminate between people on any grounds whatever.

3.4. Before discussing other possible rules let us first consider the arguments that might be adduced in favour of the 'standard' rule being the rule to be *chosen,* rather than it merely being a reference point. It has a very strong non-discriminatory egalitarian flavour, it is free of judgments about people's worth, or deserts, or influence, or likeability, or appearance, or smell, or manners, or age, sex, wealth, social class, religious beliefs, race, colour, temperament, sexual orientation, or general or particular life style. It seems *prima facie* very close to the official medical ethic when it comes to dealing with people.

3.5. Before I go any further let me dispose of a red herring which is sure to be drawn across our path sooner or later, namely that the distribution of health benefits should be determined by 'need'. I long ago argued that the most plausible interpretation of what people intend to convey in the health care context by appealing to the notion of need is that someone would be better off *with* the 'needed' treatment than *without* it.[5] This leaves open the issue of whose values determine whether (and to what extent) that person *will* be better off, and, more to the point in the present context, how one person's 'needs' (i.e. potential benefits) are to be weighed against another's.[6] So all in all an appeal to the notion of need is but a detour which leads us back to the main issue, which is, how a benefit to one kind of person is to be valued relatively to that same benefit to another kind of person.

3.6. Let us consider *age* as a fairly straightforward and obvious candidate for consideration. The classic argument is based on the 'good innings' analogy, i.e. someone who has had their three-score-years-and-ten has had a good run for their money, and precedence should be given to younger people who have not yet had a fair share of the action. The consequences of such a rule, compared with the standard rule, will obviously be an explicit discrimination *against* the old and *in favour* of the young (and, so long as women are living longer than men, it will

---

[5] See Alan Williams, 'Need as a Demand Concept (with special reference to health)', in A. J. Culyer (ed.), *Economic Policies and Social Goals* (Martin Robertson, 1974), 60–76.

[6] D. Wiggins and S. Dirmen, 'Needs, Need, Needing', *Journal of Medical Ethics* **13** (1987), 63–68, make a similar point when they concur in E. D. Watts view that 'it can make good sense to speak of needs without implying any active obligation on the part of any person to meet these needs'.

discriminate *incidentally* against women *as a group,* even though *on an age standardized basis* there would be no such sex discrimination).

3.7. Let us next consider *family responsibilities* (e.g. looking after young children or elderly relatives) as the basis of a distributive rule. If this were to count, it will favour mainly people in their twenties and thirties (as child carers) and mainly people in their forties to sixties (as carers of the elderly). With present patterns of role division, married (and some single) women will be the main beneficiaries of such a rule. But is earning money to keep the household going also a family responsibility? If so the consequences become more blurred, except that single-person households will lose out even more clearly. How narrowly or broadly drawn should this notion of family responsibilities be? And is the motivation for *this* discrimination perhaps the thought that by keeping the 'carer' healthy we are more likely to keep the 'dependants' healthy, so it is really a matter of using the higher value attributed to the benefit to the 'patient' as a proxy for a *sum* of benefits to several people? If so, would it not be better to count the benefits to the different people *directly* instead of tampering with the relative valuations? A final complicating thought here is whether this notion of 'dependency' should be extended outside the family or household, e.g. into the workplace, or into any other social setting in which people play a role which is highly valued *by other people*.

3.8. This then shades into judgments of *social worth* as a possible basis for a distribution rule. Is a great artist or performer, whose talents are widely appreciated, to be given precedence over an easily replaceable nonentity? How are such judgments to be made? Although in the (admittedly small sample of) writings on ethics I have encountered, this elitist notion is viewed with great suspicion, it is formally entrenched in the health care systems of some countries, and, I suspect, more widely practised here than we care to admit, and it may well find a ready response in the population at large. I therefore think it has to be considered.

3.9. Although *willingness and ability to pay* have been formally rejected as a suitable distribution rule for the NHS, it is a nice question whether this should nevertheless be included in any survey to see whether popular opinion still supports that rejection. But there is an interesting variant which I think has to be included anyway. It seems to me that it is the differential 'ability' to pay which people find more obnoxious than the differential 'willingness' to pay, and we do accept, in the NHS, that people who are willing and able to pay high *time* prices (e.g. by waiting in GPs' surgeries or at outpatient clinics in hospitals) get better access than those who are not so willing or able to do so (e.g. consider as examples of the former group retired people with cars, and as examples of the latter group working single-parents relying on public transport). But this 'willingness to pay' concept has a more subtle non-financial interpretation as *a willingness to make sacrifices for the sake of your health,* e.g. by giving up smoking, restraining your enthusiasm for alcohol, eating sensibly, getting regular exercise, and so on. The distributional issue is then: should the health service value health benefits more highly if they accrue to people who, by their behaviour, clearly value their own health more highly? Put more bluntly, should we discriminate against heavy smokers, heavy drinkers, obese people, free-fall parachutists, unclean people, etc. . . . . Note that this is a separate issue from the undoubted fact *on the production side* that it is more costly to give an additional year of healthy life expectancy to such people. The question here is should we value that (most costly) benefit differently if people appear *from their own behaviour* not themselves to care much about their own health?

3.10. The next possible basis for a distribution rule relies not on how the individual behaves, but on the circumstances that the individual is in, these circumstances being assumed to be largely outside that individual's control. An example might be the child born into a poor family with an alcoholic unemployed father and heavy smoking mother with no ideas about proper hygiene or nutrition. Should health benefits for such infants be valued more highly than those for infants generally? And, at the later stages of life, should someone who has behaved impeccably (whatever that means substantively) with regard to their own health-related behaviour, but has been persistently unemployed, and is in poor housing in a poor physical environment, have their health benefits upvalued as some kind of compensatory mechanism for their other deprivations? To go further, does this mean generally that benefits to the poor should be valued more highly than benefits to the rich, in which case have we not reintroduced discrimination by willingness and ability to pay, but now in reverse? Nevertheless, whatever tangles we may get into over this possible dimension of discrimination, I am sure it has to be included in any survey work about possible distribution rules.

3.11. There are perhaps other important characteristics by which someone might argue that the NHS should discriminate when allocating health benefits. I have assumed that discrimination by sex, colour, race or creed is unacceptable, but if there are others I have missed I would welcome suggestions. For the time being I have been working on the following repertoire:

3.11.1. No discrimination whatever.

3.11.2. Discrimination by age (the younger the better).

3.11.3. Discrimination by family responsibilities (the more dependants the better).

3.11.4. Discrimination by social worth (the more talented the better).

3.11.5. Discrimination by own implicit value of health (the more behavioural sacrifices you make for your health the better).

3.11.6. Discrimination by socioeconomic environment (the more deprived the better).

3.11.7. Discrimination by willingness and ability to pay (the richer and keener the better) [to see what support it commands].

VI. Eliciting Preferences and Trade-offs

4.1. The simplest way into this territory seems to be to begin by asking people whether or not they think there should be discrimination on each individual dimension in turn. For instance, the questions might be posed as in Table III.

4.2. Any respondent who goes for no discrimination in every single case, and does not add a write-in candidate, is not asked any further questions, except concerning their personal background (of which more anon).

4.3. Any respondent who approves of only *one* basis for discrimination, could then be asked:

> If we could keep one [state respondents' preferred class of person; e.g. 'young person'] alive and well for an extra five years by sacrific-ing that same amount of healthy life expectancy for some [state respondents' non-preferred class of person; e.g. 'old people'] how many [old people's] health would you think it right to sacrifice in order to improve the health of one [young person]?
>
> State number ☐

4.4. If a respondent favours discrimination by more than one charac-teristic, things become much more difficult. Initially they could be asked the above preference intensity question about each nominated characteristic individually. But then we would have to face the trade-off problem since the criteria might be interdependent. Suppose three criteria were nominated, in which the preferred categories were the young, those caring for children, and the deprived, treating each characteristic as simply dichotomous (no differences of degree are admissible). Then we might initially seek a rank ordering of eight people with the following stated characteristics:

Table III

Do you think it right that in deciding which ill people should be made healthy, the NHS should show any of the following preferences. (Choose one from each group of alternatives.)

1 (A) The young should get preference over the old ☐
   (B) The old should get preference over the young ☐ Tick one
   (C) Age should make no difference ☐

2 (A) People with young children should get preference over those without ☐
   (B) Having young children should make no difference ☐ Tick one

3 (A) People looking after elderly relatives should get preference over those not doing so ☐
   (B) Looking after elderly relatives should make no difference ☐ Tick one

4 (A) The breadwinner of the household should get preference over the others ☐
   (B) Being the breadwinner should make no difference ☐ Tick one

5 (A) Someone who has a lot to contribute to the community should get preference over someone who has little to offer ☐
   (B) How talented you are should make no difference ☐ Tick one

6 (A) People who have taken care of their own health should get preference over those who haven't ☐
   (B) People who have not taken much care of their own health should get preference over those who have ☐ Tick one
   (C) Whether or not you have cared for your own health should make no difference ☐

7 (A) People who are deprived in other ways should get preference when it comes to health ☐
   (B) People who are not deprived in other ways should get preference when it comes to health ☐ Tick one
   (C) Whether or not you are deprived in other ways should make no difference when it comes to health ☐

8 (A) People who are willing and able to pay part of the costs should get preference over those who are not ☐

(B) People who are not willing or able to pay part of the costs should get preference over those who are ☐ Tick one

(C) Whether or not you are willing and able to pay should make no difference ☐

9 (A) Are there any other grounds on which you think the NHS should give preference to one kind of person rather than another?

Yes ☐ No ☐

(B) If yes, who should get preference over whom?

[____] should get preference over [____]

(A) A deprived young person caring for children
(B) A deprived young person not caring for children
(C) A deprived old person caring for children
(D) A deprived old person not caring for children
(E) A comfortably off young person caring for children
(F) A comfortably off young person not caring for children
(G) A comfortably off old person caring for children
(H) A comfortably off old person not caring for children

For such a respondent Person (A) should be the most preferred, and Person (H) the least, but it is not clear *a priori* how the others will be ranked. From the earlier question about preference intensity (for each dimension separately) we should get some clues about the relative weights likely to be given to the different elements when combined, but we cannot assume that this combined weight will be related to the individual weights in any simple way, because the combination of being deprived *and* coping with young children may be regarded as attracting much greater priority than the sum of the two characteristics in isolation. I would prefer to test this directly by giving respondents some magnitude estimation task at this stage, but so far have failed to come up with one that is readily comprehensible and easily do-able by ordinary people.

4.5. Assuming that I eventually find a way through that, the only other data I will need from respondents is background about themselves, so that I can explore whether any differences that emerge in people's response patterns are systematically related to anything about them or their situation. For this purpose I need to know their age, sex,

Table IV. *Pilot survey respondents*

Occupational group	Number of different discriminations favoured					
	0	1	2	3	4	5
18 clinical psychologists	7	4	4	1	2	0
18 hospital doctors	6	3	4	2	3	0
16 secretaries	8	4	3	0	0	1
12 NHS managers	5	4	1	1	1	0
10 academics	3	1	3	1	1	1
5 nurses	2	1	2	0	0	0
2 others	1	1	0	0	0	0
81 Totals	32	18	17	5	7	2
Total number of discriminations 105 =	0 +	18 +	34 +	15 +	28 +	10

household composition and their role in it, whether caring for anyone outside the household, current employment status, current or previous occupation, educational level, religious beliefs, recent experience of illness, smoking and drinking behaviour, main recreation pursuits, housing tenure, household income, attitudes to private health insurance, etc.

V. Some Preliminary Results

5.1. I had an opportunity, at the conference at which a preliminary version of this paper was given (essentially sections I–III), to try out my questionnaire on the participants, about two-thirds of whom responded. Later I did the same at meetings of health service managers, hospital doctors, and clinical psychologists. In order to get the views of a group of people closer to the ordinary citizenry, I finally tried out my questionnaire (as in Table III, but with a lot of background data also elicited) on a group of secretaries within the University. This pilot study generated the pattern of responses in Table IV: i.e. 1·3 discriminations per person overall, or 2·1 per person who discriminates at all. It will be noted that just under forty per cent of the respondents favour no discrimination whatever, and, of the five occupational groups with the larger number of respondents, this non-discriminatory view was strongest amongst the secretaries and weakest amongst the doctors and the academics (most of the latter being philosophers of one kind or another).

5.2. But what is rather more interesting is the *choice* of discriminators. This is set out in Table V:

123

Table V. Choice of discriminators by occupational group

| | Frequency of mention | | | | | | | |
	Young	With children	Elderly relatives	Bread- winner	Social contribution	Careful of health	Deprived	Will pay
Psychologists	5	6	3	1	1	5	2	0
Doctors	5	6	4	3	3	7	1	0
Secretaries	3	3	6	1	1	1	0	0
Managers	5	1	2	1	1	3	0	0
Academics	6	4	1	0	2	4	1	1
Nurses	1	0	0	0	0	2	1	1
Others	0	0	0	0	0	1	0	0
Totals 105:	25	20	16	6	8	23	5	2

It is the first three axes of possible discrimination plus being careful over your own health, which clearly dominate, but this frequency count may be rather misleading, because it contains five 'votes' from some people, and only one from others (see Table IV), and none, of course, from the non-discriminators.

5.3. If the data in Table V are reworked to allow each (discriminating) person only one vote (so that if someone votes for two items, each item counts ½, and a three item vote counts ⅓ each, and so on) then we get the 'adjusted' distribution of votes as set out in Table VI.

This obviously changes the rank ordering slightly, but it highlights some other interesting features. For instance, the secretaries are especially concerned with those caring for elderly relatives, the doctors strongly favour those who have taken care of their own health, and the psychologists, managers and the academics tend to support discrimination in favour of the young over the old, as can be seen when these same data are reworked as in Table VII. But to explore these phenomena more closely we need to delve rather more deeply into the background data.

5.4. If we look first at the respondents who support discrimination in favour of *those who have taken care of their own health,* there was no

Table VI. Adjusted choice of discriminators by occupational group

	Young	With children	Elderly relatives	Bread- winner	Social contribution	Careful of health	Deprived	Will pay
Psychologists	3·3	2·8	1·0	0·3	0	2·8	0·8	0
Doctors	1·6	1·9	1·3	0·8	1·3	4·7	0·5	0
Secretaries	1·2	1·2	4·2	0·2	0·2	1·0	0	0
Managers	3·1	0·3	0·6	0·3	0·3	2·5	0	0
Academics	2·3	1·5	0·2	0	0·6	1·8	0·2	0·5
Nurses	1·0	0	0	0	0	1·0	0·5	0·5
Others	0	0	0	0	0	1·0	0	0
Totals 49·3:	12·5	7·7	7·3	1·6	2·4	14·8	2·0	1·0

Table VII. Adjusted choice of discrimination by main occupational groups standardized so that each now sums to 100

	Young	With children	Elderly relatives	Bread-winner	Social contribution	Careful of health	Deprived	Will pay
Psychologists	30	25	9	3	0	25	7	0
Doctors	13	16	11	7	11	39	4	0
Secretaries	15	15	53	3	3	13	0	0
Managers	44	4	8	4	4	35	0	0
Academics	32	21	3	0	8	25	3	7
Overall*	25	16	15	3	5	30	4	2

*Includes nurses and others, for whom the number of observations are too small to warrant a separate entry.

noticeable age or sex effect here, nor did those supporting this kind of discrimination do more things themselves for the sake of their own health than the others did. What *was* very noticeable, however, was that whilst similar proportions of ex-smokers and never-smokers supported this kind of discrimination, not a single one of the twelve current smokers did.

5.5. A rather more surprising result from my respondents was that those *favouring the young over the old* were predominantly the old. But those favouring discrimination in favour of *those looking after elderly relatives* did not have more elderly persons in their households, though they were predominantly women, and especially women over forty. But the group most favouring discrimination in favour of *those looking after young children* were the older *males,* though here there was an even stronger correlation with the number of children in the household (those in favour had 1·2 children per household, those against only 0·6 children per household).

5.6. In this pilot survey the self-reported state of people's own health, having had any recent consultations with doctors, and whether or not a religious person, had no significant effect on responses. Too few people had low incomes or poor educational qualification for this to be tested as an explanatory variable. And it need hardly be said that this sample, being small and unrepresentative, cannot be taken to reflect the views of the Great British Public.

5.7. It does however indicate the rich vein of material to be mined in this territory, about which we know very little, despite its rather crucial policy importance. It strongly suggests that although the most common single view may well be that the NHS should not discriminate at all between people when it comes to distributing the benefits of health care, there are just as many people who favour discrimination by more than one criterion (there are thirty-two of the former and thirty-one of the latter in Table IV). Nor, on this limited evidence, is there much support for the view that doctors (and to some extent the managers), who at present are the ones left to exercise such discrimination as occurs, do accurately reflect the views of the rest of the population. Clearly there is a substantial research task to be undertaken here . . . and we have not started on the trade-off problem yet.

Index of Names

Index of Subjects